ADDITIVE AND NONADDITIVE MEASURES OF ENTROPY

M. Behara
McMaster University and Institutum Gaussianum

JOHN WILEY & SONS
New York   Chichester   Brisbane   Toronto   Singapore

First Published in 1990
WILEY EASTERN LIMITED
4835/24 Ansari Road, Daryaganj
New Delhi-110 002, India

Distributors :

Australia and New Zealand
JACARANDA WILEY LTD.
P O Box 1226, Milton Old 4064, Australia

Canada :
JOHN WILEY & SONS LIMITED
22 Worcester Road, Rexdale, Ontario, Canada

Europe and Africa :
JOHN WILEY & SONS LIMITED
Baffins Lane, Chichester, West Sussex, England

South East Asia :
JOHN WILEY & SONS (PTE) LTD.
05-04, Block B, Union Industrial Building
37 Jalan Pemimpin, Singapore 2057

Africa and South Asia :
WILEY EASTERN LIMITED
4835/24 Ansari Road, Daryaganj
New Delhi-110 002, India

North and South America and rest of the world :
JOHN WILEY & SONS, INC.
605, Third Avenue, New York, NY 10158 USA

ISBN 0-470-21728-6 John Wiley & Sons, Inc.
ISBN 81-224-0257-7 Wiley Eastern Limited

Printed in India at Raj Bandhu Industrial Company, New Delhi.

ADDITIVE AND NONADDITIVE MEASURES OF ENTROPY

To

Günter Menges

IN MEMORIAM

CONTENTS

PREFACE

The purpose of this research monograph is to present a unified theory of measures of entropy developed during the past two decades. I conceived the idea of parabolic entropy in 1965. I did my research on this generalized entropy and its application in decision and coding theories during my visit, for a semester, to Cornell University in 1966 at the invitation of the late Professor Jacob Wolfowitz. I have benefited greatly by my continued close personal association with Jack ever since. In 1968, I presented my results in an invited paper at Oberwolfach. As in my dissertation written under the late Professor Günter Menges, the relationship between entropy and utility in decision theory was again established, this time using the parabolic entropy which is endowed with a parameter. After completing his post—doctoral fellowship under Professor J. Aczel, Dr. Prem Nath joined me in the same capacity, and together we wrote our forty—two page long report on *Additive and Non—Additive Measures of Entropy* in 1970, the summary of which appeared in Mathematical Reviews soon after. When I discovered a two—page account of parabolic entropy in the highly recognized text on Information Theory by S. Guiasu in 1977, I was tempted to publish my monograph immediately afterwards. However, believing that it was imperative to include results on algebraic and transcendental entropies in my monograph, I withheld its publication until now. I realize that a book is never written in the final form, and that is why, for over two years now, Professor Kannappan and I have been working on a sequel to the monograph with applications in Ergodic Theory, Statistics, Economics, Pattern Recognition and Decision Sciences.

Only rudiments of additive measures of entropy are given here to serve as an introduction and historical completion to the main part of the monograph on measures of nonadditive entropy and its applications in coding theory. The concept of geometric entropy has its roots in parabolic entropy. The idea is simply to discover new measures of entropy from geometric configurations in the same manner as a certain parabola literally defines the parabolic entropy. The theory obviously needs generalizations in three and higher dimensions. In a similar vein, certain mathematical functions, when subjected to axioms of information measures, could give rise to measures of entropies. Algebraic and transcendental entropies derived this way, as well as geometric entropies, form the foundation of the unified theory of entropy measures. Detailed classifications of entropy measures, according to geometric and functional (algebraic and transcendental) criteria will facilitate the study of their properties. Parametric entropies such as the Rényi, an additive measure and the Polynomial, which is a nonadditive measure, are naturally much richer than a nonparametric one such as the Shannon entropy. Professor J. M. S. Chawla, presently at Acadia University, demonstrated the usefulness of a parametric entropy in ergodic theory in his Ph.D. thesis, which was written under my supervision at McMaster. I think that parametric entropies can be used in extracting a sharper image in pattern recognition theory. Similarly, nonadditive measures of entropy may be used in restructuring the theory of design and analysis of experiments. Professor E. Kofler of the University of Zürich and I have been involved in the applications of parametric entropy in fuzzy set theory and forecasting problems in economics. A wealth of untapped research resources is inherent in the study of coding theory based on nonadditive entropies. There are various other measures, such as divergence, which are derived from measures of entropy and which can now be formulated with higher sensitivity in a more general setting. The range of applications of parametric, and in particular of nonadditive entropies, in virtually every field of human knowledge where measurement of the amount of information or uncertainty is essential, has no end in sight. In short, nonadditive measures of entropy are much more adaptable to real world situations, whereas a crude and unsophisticated measure, such as the Shannon entropy, has only limited applications.

In this work, I have had no opportunity to touch on my favourite area of research, the ever futuristic field of decision theory which I embarked upon in the early sixties. Since then, my almost continuous discussions with my mentor and unforgettable friend Günter Menges on practically every aspect related to information and decision sciences (and arts!) abruptly ended with his sudden and very untimely death in 1983. This modest contribution is dedicated to his memory.

ACKNOWLEDGEMENTS

I wish to express my deep gratitude towards Dr. J. Aczel, F.R.S.C., Distinguished Professor of Pure Mathematics as well as to Dr. PL. Kannappan, Professor of Pure Mathematics, both of the University of Waterloo, for their detailed and critical examination of the entire manuscript and for their invaluable help in suggesting any necessary improvements. Needless to say the responsibility for any inaccuracies or omissions is entirely my own.

Many thanks are due to Professor P. Nath of the University of Delhi and the University of Mauritius, Professor N.S. Kambo, Head of the Mathematics Department at IIT,

Delhi and Dr P.N. Arora of the University of Delhi for reading the manuscript and for over two decades worth of stimulating discussions concerning information theory.

Professor L.L. Campbell, Head of the Department of Mathematics and Statistics at Queen's University and Professor Jaya Srivastava of Colorado State University, were kind enough to write forewords to earlier versions of the monograph which were completed before 1981, for which I am very thankful.

For the large amount of computer work related to the monograph I am greatly indebted to my son Max.

I am grateful to Mr. A. Machwe and Mr. H.S. Poplai of Wiley Eastern for their encouragement and patience with this project.

Parts of the monograph were written and tested on my students while I held several visiting professorships including the Richard Merton Professorship at the University of Heidelberg, to which I owe my gratitude.

PART ZERO

INTRODUCTION

0.0 AMOUNT OF INFORMATION

Boltzmann (1896), in his "Vorlesungen über Gastheorie" laid the foundation of the probabilistic theory of entropy.

Wiener (1948) and Shannon (1948) are credited for the development of a quantitative measure, provided by a probabilistic experiment, of the amount of information, known as Shannon entropy or simply entropy in the literature. Shannon entropy may be considered as a generalization of the definition of entropy given by Hartley (1928) where probability of each event is equal and, hence, may also be regarded, as a non—probabilistic measure of entropy.

Now, in the fleeting span of less than half—a—century of active participation by the scientists in the theory of information, its investigators have settled into two major realms of concentration. American mathematicians on the one hand have primarily concerned themselves with such aspects of the theory as stronger theorems concerning the existence of codes and their algebraic structures, and perhaps even more emphatically with the relatively practical considerations of actual codes constructions. Other researchers, predominantly Soviet, have been principally engaged in the problems of the theory of transmission of signals of an arbitrary nature, a problem which then readily lends itself to the problem of extending the basic concepts of information theory to general probabilistic schemes. Golay (1949) and Hamming (1950) discovered the first algebraic codes known as Hamming Codes while Shannon coding theorems prove the existence of codes with large rate of transmission and less errors. The construction of balanced incomplete block designs by Bose (1939) may be regarded as a forerunner of the algebraic theory of error—correcting codes. Khinchin (1953) gave the first clear and rigorous presentation of the mathematical foundations of the concept of entropy.

The discipline of information theory in both its areas of entropy and error—correcting codes has grown tremendously ever since. The purpose of this work is to discuss the mathematical theory of various measures of the amount of information and some of its applications.

There are two approaches, pragmatic and axiomatic, by means of which the mathematical theory concerning various measures of the amount of information can be developed. These two approaches seem to be entirely different from each other but, in reality, they are complimentary to each other. In the pragmatic approach, we seek to formulate certain particular problems of information theory and then accept as the amount of information those mathematical quantities which present themselves in their solutions. Here, we propose a novel method of using mathematical functions or their geometric configurations in the derivations of the measures of information. This approach is due to Behara (1968). See also Behara and Nath (1973). The fact that the classical measure of information, the Shannon entropy is encountered in solving a large number of father different problems is suggestive of the fact that it is a fundamental notion. In this case, we naturally attempt to understand why this same quantity occurs in different contexts, that is, to determine just which are its properties which make it so useful, and this is exactly the aim of the second, the axiomatic approach. This axiomatic approach is, then, motivated in an attempt to formulate those properties which a reasonable measure of information is supposed to satisfy. The postulational statement of these particular properties is, in turn, an interpretation of more fundamental properties justified at an intuitive level of understanding of the problem. The subsequent step of this approach leads to the purely mathematical question which must be solved to determine all the expressions which possess the postulated properties. A fundamental requirement in the axiomatic approach is to devise a set of axioms such that no two axioms overlap each other.

Whether, at any stage in the investigation, we are prepared to be purely deductive or not is a question difficult to answer but we are inevitably interested in such a unification is undoubtedly clear. These two approaches, nevertheless, complement each other in the sense that they may and should be used as controls for one another.

The axiomatic approach attempts to formulate a postulational system which, apparently, provides a unique numerical characteristic which adequately reflects the properties required of an information function in a diverse real situation. This axiomatic approach is generally maintained to be intrinsically related to the notion of entropy together with its generalizations. Alternatively, some other researchers, in particular, Wolfowitz (1957) have demonstrated that, for the study of various coding theorems concerning various noisy channels, the concept of entropy may be considered in an auxiliary role as a quantity and may preferably be replaced by certain combinatorial arguments.

Essentially, we begin with the very plausible assumption that information is a measurable entity so that it is desirable to have means of measuring the amount of information present in a given situation. Given this not unreasonable assumption, our problem is to set up, if possible, some quantitative measures by means of which the capacities of various communication systems to transmit information may be compared. In estimating the capacity of a communication system to transmit information, we ignore the question of interpretation, make the selection of each message to be transmitted such that it is leased on some statistical rule and base our results only on the possibility of the receiver distinguishing the result of selecting any one symbol from that of selecting any other. By these means, we attempt to eliminate the psychological vagaries of a given situation, thereby, rendering feasible the formulation of a definite quantitative measure of information based on physical considerations. This problem is, of course, originally a physical one, and consequently, we must pay our attention to the relevant boundary conditions in our mathematical interpretations.

At the outset of our considerations, we must conform ourselves to a definitive meaning of the term *"information"* This is essential because whenever a word of common usage is taken into a scientific discipline, its meaning has to be specified very precisely. Below, we explain the sense in which we shall use the term information:

By the word *information* we shall simply mean a mere collection of facts. To obtain the facts, one has to have some sort of experiment in mind. We assign first a numerical *uncertainty* value to an experiment prior to actually performing an experiment, at which time the result of the experiment is yet unknown. Before proceeding further, we would like to say a few words regarding the notion of uncertainty. Since a measure of information or, for that matter, a measure of uncertainty is motivated for the sole purpose of comparing the information content or uncertainty stored in a set of experiments, we seek to justify the sense comparatively. If, say, we consider an experiment consisting of events of which one, in particular, occurs with a disproportionately high probability, then, in the performance of this experiment this event will occur with a high degree of uncertainty. The uncertainty associated with such an experiment will, then, very naturally be less than that stored in an experiment consisting of events all almost equally likely to occur.

Returning now to our original experimental situation, after performing the experiment we gain *information* by the realization of which of the set of possible experimental outcomes actually did occur. Moreover, we take the numerical measure of the *uncertainty*, which may be thought of as stored in the experiment prior to discovering the outcome also as the measure of the amount of *information* gained by determining the experimental outcome. The quantity *information* may also be considered as stored in the experiment and, in fact, the measure of the amount of information gained is taken numerically equal to the measure of the amount of uncertainty removed. Though the term *uncertainty* in its present usage is readily an intuitively consistent notion, the same may not necessarily be said of *information* whose conventional usage, as we shall comment upon, is strikingly different.

Furthermore, if the experiment consisted of one possible outcome which was, in fact, certain to occur, then we naturally claim no uncertainty present in the experiment and, analogously, we impose the restriction on our terminology that no *information* can be obtained by performing an experiment in which a particular outcome occurs with probability one.

Though perhaps the choice of the phrase *amount of information*, also known as entropy, may appear to have tenuous connection to its usage in any ordinary sense, this is a semantic criticism, and as such is beyond our realm of investigation. Nevertheless, we note a few examples to emphasize the distinction between the conventional definition related to *meaning* and the *information—theoretic* definition of the word *information*.

Accepting information—theoretic notions would imply that if Lewis Carroll were told that his stories were improbable, he could retort by saying that they were as a result, all the more informative. Even more politically scandalous is the information–theoretic consequence that, in a sense, the solution of a mathematical problem produces no new information, thereby, consequently bringing the danger that the general public might be led to conclude from this that mathematicians do no useful work. Due to these conflicts of views, we must then simply bear in mind the distinction between information and uncertainty while studying the theory of information transmission. Finally, though protests against the apparent misuse of the English language are, perhaps. to some extent justifiable if the word *information* had not already long ago caught on among the electrical engineers, it would likely not have been used in favour of one perhaps more intuitively consistent.

0.1 STATISTICAL PRELIMINARIES

By a *random experiment* or *simply an experiment*, we shall always mean a situation depending on chance. The set of all possible outcomes of an experiment is called the *sample space* of that experiment. Let Ω denote the sample space of a random experiment. A non—empty class $\mathfrak{B}$ of subsets of Ω is called a *Boolean* $\sigma-algebra$ if it is closed under complementation and countable unions. The pair $(\Omega, \mathfrak{B})$ is called a *measurable space*. By a probability measure μ, we shall always mean a mapping $\mu: \mathfrak{B} \to [0,1]$ such that $\mu(\Omega) = 1$ and μ

is a countably additive set function. The triple $(\Omega,\mathfrak{B},\mu)$ is called a *probability space*. The elements of $\mathfrak{B}$ are called μ–measurable sets and $\mu(E)$ is called the *probability* of $E \in \mathfrak{B}$.

Let $\Omega_1 \in \mathfrak{B}$ with $\mu(\Omega_1) > 0$. A mapping $\xi: \Omega_1 \to \mathbb{R}$, $\mathbb{R} = (-\infty,+\infty)$, is called a *generalized random variable* if the inverse image of each Borel subset of $\mathbb{R}$ is an element of $\mathfrak{B}$. In other words, ξ is a $\mathfrak{B}$–measurable real–valued function. If $\mu(\Omega_1) = 1$, then ξ is called a *complete random variable*. If $0 < \mu(\Omega_1) < 1$, then ξ is called an *incomplete random variable*. According to Rényi (1960), an incomplete random variable can be regarded as quantity describing the result of a random experiment all of whose events are not observable so that its sample space is some *measurable subset* $\Omega_1 \in \mathfrak{B}$ with $0 < \mu(\Omega_1) < 1$.

Let us suppose that ξ takes only a finite number of distinct real values, say, $x_1, x_2, ..., x_n$, $n \geq 1$. Since ξ is a generalized random variable, therefore, by definition, each inverse image $\xi^{-1}(\{x_k\}), k = 1, 2, ..., n$; belongs to $\mathfrak{B}$ and hence it is an event because the singleton sets $\{x_k\}, k = 1, 2, ..., n$; are Borel subsets of $R = (-\infty,+\infty)$. Consequently, we can talk of the probabilities

$$\mu(\xi^{-1}\{x_k\}) = p_k \geq 0, k = 1, 2, ..., n, \; 1 \geq \sum_{i=1}^{n} p_i > 0.$$

A finite generalized probability distribution is a vector of the form

$$p = (p_1, p_2, ..., p_n), \ p_k \leq 0, \ 0 < \sum_{k=1}^{n} p_k \leq 1.$$

The quantity $W(P) = \sum_{k=1}^{n} p_k$ is called the *weight* of the probability distribution P associated with the generalized random variable ξ. If $0 < \sum_{k=1}^{n} p_k < 1$, then the probability distribution $P = (p_1, p_2, ..., p_n)$ is called an *incomplete probability distribution*. If $\sum_{k=1}^{n} p_k = 1$, then P is called a *complete probability distribution*.

Since the value $x_1, x_2, ..., x_n$, $n \geq 1$, taken by the generalized variable ξ are distinct, therefore, the inverse images $\xi^{-1}\{x_k\}$, $k = 1, 2, ...$, are distinct $\mathfrak{B}$—measurable sets which are non—empty and whose union equals $\Omega_1 \epsilon \mathfrak{B}$. We shall say that these inverse images form a *measurable partition* of Ω_1. By the above considerations, it is clear that, to each measurable partition of Ω_1, there corresponds a generalized probability distribution. Hence, different measurable partitions of Ω_1 will give rise to different generalized probability distributions and consequently it is desirable to introduce the following notation:

$$\Delta_n = \begin{cases} (p_1, p_2, ..., p_n) : p_k \geq 0, \ k = 1, 2, ..., n; \\ \\ 0 < \sum_{k=1}^{n} p_k \leq 1, \ n = 1, 2, ... \end{cases}$$

Let $\Delta' = \bigcup_{n=1}^{\infty} \Delta_n'$. Obviously, Δ' denotes the set of *all possible generalized discrete probability distributions.*

If $n = 1$, the generalized probability distribution

$$P = \{(p), 0 < p \leq 1\},$$

is called a *generalized singleton probability distribution.*

For the sake of convenience, let us also introduce the notations:

$$\Delta_n = \begin{cases} (p_1, p_2, ..., p_n): p_k \geq 0, k = 1, 2, ... n; \\ \sum_{k=1}^{n} p_k = 1, n = 1, 2, ...; \Delta = \bigcup_{n=1}^{\infty} \Delta_n. \end{cases}$$

Clearly, Δ denotes the set of *all possible complete discrete probability distributions* and consequently $\Delta' - \Delta$ is the set of *all possible incomplete discrete probability distributions.*

In practice, one has often to deal with more than one experiment not necessarily having the same space and it is also possible that the occurrence of events of one experiment may effect the occurrence of events of the other experiment.

Let $(\Omega_1, \mathcal{B}_1, \mu_1)$ and $(\Omega_2, \mathcal{B}_2, \mu_2)$ be two probability spaces representing two different experiments and let $\{E_1, E_2, ..., E_n\}$

and $\{F_1, F_2, ..., F_m\}$ be the measurable partitions of Ω_1 and Ω_2, that is,

$$\begin{cases} 0 \neq E_i \in \mathfrak{B}_1, \ 0 \neq F_j \in \mathfrak{B}_2, \ i = 1,2,...,n; \ j = 1,2,...,m; \\[2ex] \bigcup_{i=1}^{n} E_i = \Omega_1, \ \bigcup_{j=1}^{m} F_j = \Omega_2. \end{cases}$$

$$\begin{cases} \text{Let } \mu_1(E_i) = p_i \geq 0, \ \mu_2(F_j) = q_j \geq 0, \\[2ex] i = 1,2,...,n; \ j = 1,2,...,m; \ \sum_{i=1}^{n} p_i = 1 = \sum_{j=1}^{m} q_j. \end{cases}$$

For the sake of simplicity, let us assume that all p_i's are positive. Suppose that the elements of $\mathfrak{B}_2$ are conditioned with respect to the elements of $\mathfrak{B}_1$. Using measure–theoretic considerations, the details of which we are omitting, one can define the *joint probability space* $(\Omega_1 \times \Omega_2. \ \mathfrak{B}_1 \times \mathfrak{B}_2, \mu_{12})$ where

$$\Omega_1 \times \Omega_2 = \{(\omega_1, \omega_2): \omega_1 \in \Omega_1, \omega_2 \in \Omega_2\}, \ \mathfrak{B}_1 \times \mathfrak{B}_2$$

is the smallest σ–algebra containing all measurable rectangles of the form $E \times F$, $E \in \mathfrak{B}_1$, $F \in \mathfrak{B}_2$ and μ_{12} is the product probability measure. Let $\mu_{12}(E_i \times F_j) = r_{ij}$, that is r_{ij} denotes the probability of simultaneous occurrence of the events $E_i \in \mathfrak{B}_1$ and $F_j \in \mathfrak{B}_2$. Then, the ratio $r_{j/1} = r_{ij}/p_i$ denotes the *conditional probability* of occurrence of the event F_j with respect to the event E_i. In this way, for a *fixed* P_i, one gets the complete probability distribution

$$\left\{\frac{r_{i1}}{p_i}, \frac{r_{i2}}{p_i}, ..., \frac{r_{im}}{p_i}\right\} \epsilon \Delta_m$$

The probability distribution

$$\{r_{11}, r_{21}, ..., r_{n1}; r_{12}, r_{22}, ..., r_{n2}; ...; r_{1m}, r_{2m}, ..., r_{nm}\} \epsilon \Delta_{nm}$$

is called the joint probability distribution. The numbers r_{ij} have the following properties:

$$\begin{cases} \sum_{i=1}^{n} r_{ij} = q_j, \ j = 1, 2, ..., m, \\ \sum_{j=1}^{m} r_{ij} = p_i, \ i = 1, 2, ..., n, \\ \sum_{i=1}^{n} \sum_{j=1}^{m} r_{ij} = 1. \end{cases}$$

In case

(1) $\qquad r_{ij} = p_i q_j, \ i=1, 2, ..., n; \ j = 1, 2, ..., m,$

we say that the probability distributions

$$P = \{p_1, p_2, ..., p_n\} \text{ and } Q = \{q_1, q_2, ..., q_m\}$$

are statistically independent.

Assuming all q_j's to be positive, the conditional

probability of E_i with respect to F_j can be defined on similar lines. In general, we have

$$(2) \qquad r_{ij} = p_i\, r_{j/i} = q_j\, r_{i/j}$$

where $r_{j/i}$ = conditional probability of F_j with respect to E_i and $r_{i/j}$ = conditional probability of E_i with respect to F_j.

0.2 INFORMATION–THEORETICAL PRELIMINARIES

Here, we shall discuss some information–theoretic concepts. Now–a–days, information theory is of two kinds: *probabilistic* and *non–probabilistic*. In non–probabilistic information theory, as is evident from the name itself, we do not make use of the probabilities of the events pertaining to the experiment under consideration. The development of non–probabilistic information theory is beyond the scope of this work.

In probabilistic information theory, which we study here, it is assumed that the amount of information obtained by the occurrence of an event is *only a function of its probability of occurrence*. Since information gained is uncertainty removed, therefore, implicitly, we are indeed assuming the intrinsic association of the notion of probability with that of uncertainty. During the past few years, researchers in information theory have been busy in investigating the relationships between the notions of *probability* and *information*. We do not go into these details here. However, it would be appropriate to mention that *probability* of occurrence of an event can also be regarded as a function of the amount of *information* yielded by that event.

The primary question in the probabilistic information theory is the following: Suppose we have an experiment with mutually exclusive events

$$\begin{bmatrix} E_1, E_2, ..., E_n; \ n \geq 1, \ E_i \cap E_j \neq \phi, \ E_i \neq \phi, \\ \\ i, j = 1, 2, .., n; \bigcup_{i=1}^{n} E_i = \Omega \end{bmatrix}$$

where Ω denotes the sample space. Suppose the probabilities of these events are given by the probability distribution

$$P = (p_1, p_2, ..., p_n); \ P_i \geq 0, \ i = 1, 2, ..., n, \ \sum_{i=1}^{n} p_i = 1.$$

How much information do we obtain on the average when any one of these mutually exclusive events occurs? It is clear that, to answer this question, we need a real—valued function H with domain Δ such that $H(p_1,p_2,...,p_n)$ denotes the average amount of information gained or the average amount of uncertainty removed when any one of the events with probabilities

$$p_i \geq 0,\ i = 1,2,...,n,\ \sum_{i=1}^{n} p_i = 1,$$

occurs. To be more precise, it is better to write $H(p_1,p_2,...,p_n)$ as $H_n(p_1,p_2,...,p_n)$ to exhibit the dependence on n, the number of events in the experiment.

The function $H_n;\ \Delta_n \rightarrow R$ has been subjected to much scrutiny and several popular axiomatic formulations have been proposed to uniquely characterize it, particularly, in its classical form, called the Shannon entropy. (The choice of the term *Entropy* recalls its similarity in form — in the case of *Shannon entropy* — with an identically named quantity of fundamental importance in thermodynamical considerations).

Shannon (1948) came across the classical quantity, now—a—days, commonly known as the Shannon entropy in communication theory. In the simplest communication model, the first thing which we need is a *source* which gives us information to be communicated. Let us consider only those sources whose alphabets are finite sets. Whatsoever be the actual nature and structure of the elements of a source álphabet, we can always assign them some symbols and hence we may denote the alphabet of any source having n distinct symbols by the finite set $A_n = \{a_1, a_2, ..., a_n\}$. We assume the source to be memoryless so that it emits various symbols of its alphabet without any interdependence between the symbols already emitted by it. A finite sequence consisting of elements of source alphabet $A_n = \{a_1, a_2, ..., a_n\}$ is called a *message*. Sometimes, it is necessary to transform the original form of the messages into another new form which is acceptable to the channel, i.e., a medium for transmitting the coded messages. The process of transforming the messages into a new form acceptable to the channel is called *coding* or *encoding*. The new alphabet needed to code the messages is called the code alphabet which we may denote by the finite set $\Gamma = \{\alpha_1, \alpha_2, ..., \alpha_D\}$, $D \geq 2$. The coded messages are then transmitted over a channel. During the transmission, the coded messages get *corrupted* with unwanted disturbances called *noise* which has its statistical character. After the transmission is over, the contaminated received form of the coded messages is decoded into the original form of the messages and then carried over to the destination. It is clear that the input alphabet of the channel has to be the code alphabet

$$\Gamma = \{\alpha_1, \alpha_2, ..., \alpha_D\}, D \geq 2;$$

but the output alphabet of the channel may be a different finite set, say,

$$\Gamma' = \{\beta_1, \beta_2, ..., \beta_{D'}\}, \; D' \geq 2,$$

and it is not necessary for the sets Γ and Γ' to have the same cardinality.

After the symbol α_i is transmitted, a symbol β_j is obtained at the output end of the channel with probability $p(\beta_j/\alpha_i)$. Since α_i will be received as some β_j, $j = 1, 2, ..., D'$, therefore, we must have $\sum_j p(\beta_j/\alpha_i) = 1$. Depending upon a β_j received. we might also like to know as to which α_i was sent and since there must exist one and only one such α_i, we must have $\sum_i p(\alpha_i/\beta_j) = 1$. Clearly, this can be done only if $D' \geq D$. To accomplish such an assignment of α_i's to β_j's, normally, what we do is that we define a decision scheme as a partition of the set Γ' into D mutually disjoint non—empty subsets B_i, $i = 1, 2, ..., D$; $\bigcup_{i=1}^{D} B_i = \Gamma$ such that if the received $\beta_j \; \epsilon \; B_i$, then the decision is that α_i was transmitted.

We are interested in the amount of uncertainty or the amount of information transmitted in this process. Clearly, in order to know the amount of information transmitted through the channel, we must know two things: (a) the total amount of information available at the input end of the channel or, equivalently, the total amount of uncertainty available at the input end of the channel, (b) the amount of uncertainty still prevalent at the input end of the channel after all the output symbols have been observed. In case of (a), we need to know the probabilities of various elements of Γ. The picking up of a symbol from Γ may be regarded as an experiment such that $p(\alpha_i)$ denotes the probability of α_i being picked up. Thus, the average uncertainty at the input end is

$$H_D[p(\alpha_1),p(\alpha_2),...,p(\alpha_D)].$$

The average amount of uncertainty associated with the input end of the channel when any symbol at the output end is observed is the conditional uncertainty

$$H_{D,D'}(p(\alpha_1),p(\alpha_2),...,p(\alpha_D)/p(\beta_1),p(\beta_2),...,p(\beta_{D'})).$$

The amount of information transmitted by the channel is the defined as

$$\begin{bmatrix} I(P;Q) = H_D[p(\alpha_1),p(\alpha_2),...,p(\alpha_D)] \\ - H_{D,D'}[\{p(\alpha_1),p(\alpha_2),...,p(\alpha_D)\}/\{p(\beta_1),p(\beta_2),...,p(\beta_{D'})\}] \end{bmatrix}$$

$$= H_D(P) - H_{D,D'}(P/Q)$$

where

$$P = [p(\alpha_1),p(\alpha_2),...,(p(\alpha_D)]$$
$$Q = [p(\beta_1),p(\beta_2),...,p(\beta_{D'})].$$

(The meaning of conditional entropy will be explained later on). Equivalently stated, if α_i is transmitted, then the degree of uncertainty with which α_i will be identified by the receiver is given by the measure of uncertainty I(P; Q).

The quantity I(P; Q) is often known as the *transinformation* of the channel and is of great importance from communication point of view. Referring to the source with finite alphabet $A_n = \{a_1, a_2, ..., a_n\}$, we can talk of the source entropy provided we know $p(a_i)$, $i = 1, 2, ..., n$, the probabilities of various letters of source alphabet A_n. In the case of non—deterministic sources, there do exist methods by means of which the probabilities of various letters can be determined. Consequently, $H_n[p(a_1), p(a_2), ..., p(a_n)]$ is the average amount of information obtained when the source emits any one of the letters of its alphabet.

So far, we have formulated various ideas only for complete probability distributions. It is natural to extent the concept of entropy and other information—theoretic concepts when the probability distributions under consideration are not necessarily complete.

0.3 ENTROPY FUNCTIONS

Our object, here, is to discuss various properties which the entropy function $H_n: \Delta_n' \to \mathbb{R}$ is supposed to satisfy intuitively. Later on, these properties will be used in various axiomatic characterizations of H_n, $n = 1,2,3,...$ No claim is made of exhaustion of possible intuitively motivated properties in the following. However, the formulation of so–called intuitively motivated properties is, by its very nature, a very amorphous enterprise indeed; and such a consideration is intended purely for heuristic reasons.

(i) *Non−negativity*: It is natural to assume that in any experimental situation, we either gain some information or we do not gain any information at all. Interpreted mathematically, this amounts to saying that

$$\begin{cases} H_n(p_1,p_2,...,p_n) \geq 0, \\ (p_1,p_2,...,p_n) \ \epsilon \ \Delta_n{}'. \end{cases}$$

In other words, for all positive integers $n = 1,2,...$, the function H_n is *bounded from below* by zero.

(ii) *Nullity*: If an experiment consists of an event which occurs with probability one so that all other events occur with probability zero, then there is no uncertainty inherent in such an experiment and the amount of information yielded by the performance of such an experiment is zero. If $n = 1$, then this simply means that

(1) $H_1(1) = 0.$

However, for $n \geq 2$, this simply means that

(2) $H_n(\underbrace{0,...,0}_{(i-1) \ times},1,\underbrace{0,...,0}_{(n-i) \ times}) = 0, \ 1 \leq i < n, \ n = 2,3,....$

(iii)   *Permutation−Symmetry*. For all positive integers $n \geq 2$,

(3) $\begin{cases} H_n(p_1,p_2,...,p_n) = H_n(p_{k(1)},p_{k(2)},...,p_{k(n)}), \\ (p_1,p_2,...,p_n) \in \Delta_n' \end{cases}$

here $(k(1), k(2),...,k(n))$ is a permutation of $(1,2,...,n)$. This property simply states that the average amount of information given by an event does not depend upon the order in which the events occur.

(iv) *Entropy as a Mean Value*: It is perhaps reasonable to assume that the uncertainty stored in an experiment is a function of the uncertainties associated with each of its components. In fact, we might, for example, expect that the uncertainty of an experiment be simply equal to the weighted sum of the uncertainties associated with the components of the experiment. The components, in turn, may be thought of as sub—experiments to which we may assign incomplete probability distributions. Of course, in the case of sub—experiments with corresponding incomplete probability distribution, we naturally speak of uncertainty only with respect to the occurrence of an event, although the measure of uncertainty is, of course, a function of the incomplete probability distribution assigned to this sub—experiment.

Suppose

$$P = (p_1,p_2,...,p_n), \ p_i > 0, \ 0 < \sum_{i=1}^{n} p_i \leq 1,$$

is the generalized probability distribution. Since each $p_i > 0$, therefore, each p_i can be regarded as constituting a generalized singleton probability distribution associated with a sub–experiment consisting of one event only. Then, we intuitively assume that

$$(4) \qquad H_n(p_1, p_2, \ldots, p_n) = \frac{\sum_{i=1}^{n} p_i \, H_1(p_i)}{\sum_{i=1}^{n} p_i}.$$

Let us consider an experiment to which is associated the corresponding probability distribution

$$(p_1, p_2), \; p_1 > 0, \; p_2 > 0, \; p_1 + p_2 \leq 1.$$

If p_1 is extremely small as compared with p_2, for example, say, $p_1 = 0,0001$, $p_2 = 0.99$, then it is natural to expect the occurrence of an event with probability 0,99 rather than that of the event with probability 0.0001 when the experiment is performed. Of course, the possibility of occurrence of the event with probability $p_1 = 0.0001$ cannot be ruled out. But, if it occurs, it will indeed be a great surprise. This amounts to saying that $H_1(p_1)$ will be far more than $H_1(p_2)$ whose value should be negligible because its occurrence will convey virtually negligible amount of information. On the other hand, the average amount of information $H_2(p_1, p_2)$ will also not be significantly large because, on the average, one can always predict that the event with probability p_2 will occur. This is the disadvantage because the process of taking average neutralizes the individual significance of the events. Let

$$P = (p_1, p_2, \ldots, p_n) \text{ and } Q = (q_1, q_2, \ldots, q_m)$$

be two probability distributions with positive elements such that

$$\sum_{i=1}^{n} p_i + \sum_{j=1}^{m} q_j, \leq 1.$$

It is not necessary that the elements in P and Q are distinct. We can regard

$$\begin{cases} P = (p_1) \cup (p_2) \cup \ldots \cup (p_n), \\ Q = (q_1) \cup (q_2) \cup \ldots \cup (q_m). \end{cases}$$

Note that while looking upon P as a *union* of *generalized singleton* probability distributions, an element p_1 of P if repeated, is counted as many number of times as it is repeated and the same assertion holds for Q. Keeping this in view, we define

$$P \cup Q \quad \begin{cases} = (p_1) \cup (p_2) \ldots \cup (p_n) \cup (q_1) \cup (q_2) \ldots \cup (q_m) \\ = (p_1, p_2, \ldots, p_n, q_1, q_2, \ldots, q_m) \end{cases}$$

and again, the repeated element is counted as many number of times as it occurs. Obviously, P ∪ Q will have exactly n+m elements. By (4), we have

$$H_{n+m}(P \cup Q) = H_{n+m}(p_1,p_2,...,p_n;q_1,q_2,...,q_m)$$

$$= \frac{p_1H_1(p_1)+...+p_nH_1(p_n) + q_1H_1(q_1)+...+q_mH_1(q_m)}{p_1+p_2+\cdots+p_n+q_1+q_2+\cdots+q_m}$$

$$= \frac{(\sum_{i=1}^{n} p_i)H_n(p_1,p_2,..,p_n)+(\sum_{j=1}^{m} q_j)H_m(q_1,q_2,..,q_m)}{\sum_{i=1}^{n} p_i + \sum_{j=1}^{m} q_j}$$

$$= \frac{W(P) \; H_n(P) + W(Q) \; H_m(Q)}{W(P) + W(Q)}$$

where W denotes the weight (see 0.1). Thus,

$$(5) \qquad H_{n+m}(P \cup Q) = \frac{W(P) \; H_n(P) + W(Q) \; H_m(Q)}{W(P) + W(Q)}$$

(v) (*Continuity*): If $n = 1$, then $H_1(p)$ is a continuous function of $p \in (0,1]$. For $n \geq 2$, $H_n(p_1,p_2,...,p_n)$ is a continuous function of its arguments. Note that $(p_1,p_2,...,p_n) \in \Delta_n$.

For $n \geq 2$, by definition of Δ_n', it is possible that $p_i = 0$ for some values of i, $1 \geq i \geq n$. This raises the need to assign the meaning to $H_2(p,0)$. Now, assume

$$(6) \qquad \lim_{q \to 0} H_2(p,q) = H_1(p), \; p,q \in (0,1].$$

By continuity, we have

$$H_2(p,0) = \lim_{q \to 0} H_2(p,q), p,q \, \epsilon \, (0,1].$$

Hence, it is obvious that we must have

(7) $$H_2(p,0) = \lim_{q \to 0} H_2(p,q) = H_1(p), \; p,q \, \epsilon \, (0,1].$$

In particular, for $p = 1$, we have

(8) $$H_2(1,0) = H_1(1).$$

(vi) (*Expansibility*): *For all positive integers* $n \geq 1$,

(9)
$$\begin{cases} H_{n+1}(p_1,p_2,...,p_n,0) = H_n(p_1,p_2,...,p_n), \\ (p_1,p_2,...,p_n) \, \epsilon \, \Delta_n' \end{cases}$$

This property simply states that the addition of an event occurring with zero probability does not contribute anything to the average amount of information given by an experiment.

(vii) (*Additivity*): Let us consider two experiments with probability distributions $P = (p_1,p_2,...,p_n) \, \epsilon \, \Delta_n'$ and $Q = (q_1,q_2,...,q_m) \, \epsilon \, \Delta_m'$. Suppose these experiments are independent and they are conducted simultaneously. Let r_{ij} denote the probability of simultaneous occurrence of the ith event of the first experiment and jth event of the second experiment, $i = 1,...,n$ and $j = 1,...,m$. Then $r_{ij} = p_i q_j$, $i = 1,...,n$, $j = 1,...,n$. Since the experiments are independent, it is appropriate to expect intuitively that the average amount of information obtained by simultaneously conducting the two experiments is the sum of the average amounts of information given separately by the two experiments. Symbolically, it means that

$$(10) \qquad \begin{bmatrix} H_{nm}(r_{11}, r_{12}, .., ; r_{1m}, r_{21}, r_{22}, .., , r_{2m}; .., ; r_{n1}, r_{n2}, .., , r_{nm}) \\ = H_n(p_1, p_2, ..., p_n) + H_m(q_1, q_2, .., q_m), \end{bmatrix}$$

or equivalently

$$(11) \qquad H_{nm}(P*Q) = H_n(P) + H_m(Q).$$

The notation $P*Q$ means the joint probability arising when P and Q are statistically independent.

The situation is, however, a little complicated if the two experiments under consideration are not independent. Let us suppose that the first experiment depends upon the second one. Let $r_{i/j}$ denote the conditional probability of occurrence of the ith event pertaining to the first experiment when the jth event of the second experiment has occurred with positive probability q_j. Then $(r_{1/j}, r_{2/j}, ..., r_{n/j}) \in \Delta_n$ and, consequently,

$$H_n(r_{1/j}, r_{2/j}, ..., r_{n/j})$$

denotes the conditional average amount of information obtained by the occurrence of any event of the first experiment when the jth event of the second experiment has occurred with probability q_j. Let us write

$$(12) \; H_{n,m}(P/Q) = \left[\sum_{j=1}^{m} q_j \, H_n(r_{1/j}, r_{2/j}, \ldots, r_{n/j}) \right] \Big/ \sum_{j=1}^{m} q_j.$$

Obviously, $H_{n,m}(P/Q)$ denotes the conditional average amount of information obtained by the occurrence of any of the events of the first experiment when any event of the second experiment materializes. Usually, $H_{n,m}(P/Q)$ is also called the conditional entropy of P with respect to Q. Now we can state the following:

(viii) (*Strong Additivity*): For all positive integers $n \geq 2$ and $m \geq 2$,

$$(13) \qquad \begin{aligned} & H_{nm}(r_{11}, \ldots, r_{1m}; r_{21}, \ldots, r_{2m}; \ldots; r_{n1}, \ldots, r_{nm}) \\ & = H_m(q_1, q_2, \ldots, q_m) + H_{n,m}(P/Q) \end{aligned}$$

According to this property, the average amount of information obtained by the simultaneous occurrence of two experiments, is the *sum* of the average amount of information given by the second experiment (with m events) plus the conditional average amount of information given by the first experiment (with n events) with respect to the second experiment on which the occurrence of events pertaining to the first experiment depends.

▶

The above seven properties, by no means, constitute an *exhaustive* set of intuitive properties. Whether a particular property can be regarded as an intuitive one or not is a highly subjective question. For example, it is quite justified intuitively to say or expect that the average amount of uncertainty associated with an experiment is maximum if all its events are equiprobable so that when the experiment is actually performed, one cannot guess as to which event will occur. Mathematically, it amounts to saying that

$$(14) \qquad H_n(p_1, p_2, \ldots, p_n) \leq H_n\left[\frac{\sum\limits_{i=1}^{n} p_i}{n}, \frac{\sum\limits_{i=1}^{n} p_i}{n}, \ldots, \frac{\sum\limits_{i=1}^{n} p_i}{n} \right].$$

PART ONE

MEASURES OF ADDITIVE ENTROPY

1.0 INTRODUCTION

Shannon (1948) proposed the first and the most important and definitely the simplest measure of additive entropy known as Shannon entropy or simply entropy. The measure is simply the expectation of the logarithms of probabilities associated with any experiment. As such, this measure is non—parametric. Rényi (1960) proposed the next measure of additive entropy known as entropy of order α or simply the Rényi entropy. The Rényi entropy is parametric in the sense that it provides an infinite number of measures, each depending on the parameter α, $0 < \alpha < 1$, or $\alpha > 1$. For $\alpha = 1$, however, it is identical to the Shannon entropy.

We are proposing that it should be possible to derive all measures of entropy *geometrically* or alternatively, from various mathematical functions subjected to appropriate axioms of information measures. The Shannon and the Rényi entropies belong to the class of additive transcendental entropies. As of now, nothing is known about either the method of derivation of Shannon and Rényi entropies from transcendental functions or geometrical derivation of these entropies. Besides, other significant members of the class of additive entropies are yet to be discovered.

This part, then, basically deals with the most important axiomatic characterizations of the Shannon and the Rényi entropies using the method of functional equations.

Additive measures of entropy have vast realms of applications in almost all branches of human knowledge. For some applications in economics and decision sciences, see Behara and Kofler (1982) and Behara, Kofler and Menges (1978). We are now at the threshold of a new field of exciting applications of entropy in health and computer sciences.

1.1 THE SHANNON ENTROPY

We begin with the study of some measures of entropy, that is, the measures of the average amount of information associated with an experiment. Let us suppose that the experiment under consideration consists of n possible events, with probabilities

$$p_1, p_2, ..., p_n; \ p_i \geq 0 \ (i=1,2,...,n); \ \sum_{i=1}^{n} p_i = 1.$$

Our object is to devise the mathematical forms for entropy

$H_n(p_1,p_2,...,p_n)$. To begin with, let us suppose that $H_n(p_1,p_2,...,p_n) = n$, the number of events in the experiment. Clearly, in this case, the entropy is no longer a function of probabilities. Consequently, the average amount of information given by an experiment with equally likely events is the same as that given by an experiment in which the events are the same as that given by an experiment in which the events are not equally likely. Also, for positive integral values of n and m, $nm = n+m$ if and only if $n = m = 2$, it follows that this measure is not additive to all positive integers n and m. One can easily see that

$$H_{n+1}(p_1,p_2,...,p_n,0) = n+1$$

so that

$$H_{n+1}(p_1,p_2,...,p_n,0) \neq H_n(p_1,p_2,...,p_n)$$

and thus are not expansible.

Another measure with which we may try to work is

(1) $$H_n(p_1,p_2,...,p_n) = \log_2 n.$$

This also does not take into account the probabilities of various events into consideration. Also, it is not expansible but is certainly additive. Additivity is an important intuitive requirement of a measure of information or entropy, but, by this time, now some nonadditive measures of information are also known. The nonadditive measures are much more general, at least mathematically [Behara (1985)].

If we agree for the time being to use the logarithm of the number of possible outcomes of an experiment as the measure of the amount of information stored in an experiment, then, we are able to motivate, in a simple way, what turns out to be an important probabilistic measure in the theory of information transmission, viz; the measure already mentioned before, the so—called *Shannon entropy*. We do this by considering the important special case of language texts.

Usually, the different letters of the alphabet in such texts do not appear with equal frequency. Let us suppose that $\alpha_1, \alpha_2, ..., \alpha_D$, $D \geq 2$, are distinct letters of the alphabet and they occur $n_1, n_2, ..., n_D$ times in a text of length n. Then, we have

$$\sum_{i=1}^{D} n_i = n, \quad n_i \geq 0, i = 1, 2, ..., D.$$

Then the number of such texts is N where

$$(2) \qquad N = \frac{n!}{n_1! \, n_2! \, ... \, n_D} = \frac{n!}{\prod\limits_{i=1}^{D} n_i}$$

Using the above mentioned logarithmic measure of information, the average amount of information is given by

$$(3) \qquad \log_e N = \log_e n! - \sum_{i=1}^{D} \log_e n_i!$$

Using the Sterling's approximation formula

$$\log x! \approx x \log x - x, \text{ as } 0 < x \to {}_+\infty,$$

we have, as each $n_i \to \infty$,

$$\log_e N \approx n \log_e n - n - \sum_{i=1}^{D} n_i \log_e n_i.$$

Since $\sum_{i=1}^{D} n_i = n$, therefore,

(4) $$\log_e N \approx n \log_e n - \sum_{i=1}^{D} n_i \log_e n_i.$$

Now, the ratio $\frac{n_i}{n}$ represents the probability of occurrence of the letter α_i in a sequence of length n. Let $\frac{n_i}{n} \to p_i$ as $n \to \infty$ so that p_i denotes the probability of occurrence of the letter α_i in a sequence of length n. Then, (4) gives

$$\begin{cases} \log_e N \approx n \log_e n - \sum_{i=1}^{D} n \, p_i \log_e n \, p_i, \\ (p_1, p_2, .., p_D) \in \Delta_D \end{cases}$$

which, on simplification, gives

$$\log_e N \approx - n \sum_{i=1}^{D} p_i \log_e p_i$$

so that

$$(5) \qquad \frac{\log_e N}{n} \approx H_D(p_1, p_2, \ldots, p_D).$$

where

$$(6) \qquad H_D(p_1, p_2, \ldots, p_D) = -\sum_{i=1}^{D} p_i \log_e p_i.$$

We may interpret this asymptotic result as follows: By using various letters with probabilities

$$p_1, p_2, \ldots, p_D; \ \forall \ p_i \geq 0; \ \sum_{i=1}^{D} p_i = 1,$$

the amount of information transmitted by means of any one letter of the text is simply the Shannon entropy $H_D(p_1, p_2, \ldots p_D)$.

Since the entropy function (6) is, indeed, a measure of the uncertainty stored in an experiment, we seek now to show by comparing it with the intuitive properties mentioned in 0.3.

It can be easily verified that $\lim_{x \to 0^+} x \log x = 0$. In view of this observation, it is not unreasonable to assume that $0 \log 0 = 0$. It is then readily verified that (6) satisfies (i) in 0.3. Also, one can verify that, in fact, all the other seven properties (ii) to (viii) in 0.3 are also satisfied by it. Note that in the case of the above example concerning a language text, we have $(p_1, p_2, \ldots, p_D) \ \epsilon \ \Delta_D$ and not $(p_1, p_2, \ldots, p_D) \ \epsilon \ \Delta'_D$.

1.1.1 The Fadeev Characterization

THEOREM 1 *If* H: $\Delta_n \to$ R, *for all positive integers* n = 1,2,3,..., *satisfies the following three conditions*

(a) $p \to H_2(p, 1-p)$ *is a continuous function of* $p \epsilon [0,1]$

(b) $H_n(p_1, p_2, ..., p_n) = H_n(p_{k(1)}, p_{k(2)}, ..., p_{k(n)})$,
that is, H_n *is permutation−symmetric for all positive integers* n

(c) *With* $p_n = q_1 + q_2 > 0$, *and for all positive integers* $n \geq 3$, H_n *satisfies*

(1)
$$
\begin{aligned}
&H_{n+1}(p_1, p_2, ..., p_{n-1}, q_1, q_2) \\
&= H_n(p_1, p_2, ..., p_n) + p_n H_2\left[\frac{q_1}{p_n}, \frac{q_2}{p_n}\right],
\end{aligned}
$$

then H_n *is of the form*

(A) $$H_n(p_1, p_2, ..., p_n) = -c \sum_{i=1}^{n} p_i \log_2 p_i$$

where c *is an arbitrary real constant.*

The proof of this theorem is carried out in several steps as follows:

Lemma 1. $H_2(1,0) = 0$.

Proof By condition (c), we have
$$H_3(\tfrac{1}{2},\tfrac{1}{2},0) = H_2(\tfrac{1}{2},\tfrac{1}{2}) + \tfrac{1}{2} H_2(1,0).$$
Since H_3 is symmetric in its arguments, therefore,
$$H_3(\tfrac{1}{2},\tfrac{1}{2},0) = H_3(0,\tfrac{1}{2},\tfrac{1}{2}).$$
Now, by (c)
$$H_3(0,\tfrac{1}{2},\tfrac{1}{2}) = H_2(0,1) + H_2(\tfrac{1}{2},\tfrac{1}{2}).$$
Hence, equating the two values of $H_3(\tfrac{1}{2},\tfrac{1}{2},0)$. we get
$$\tfrac{1}{2} H_2(1,0) = H_2(0,1).$$
By symmetry,
$$H_2(0,1) = H_2(1,0).$$
Consequently,
$$\tfrac{1}{2} H_2(1,0) = H_2(1,0)$$
from which it follows that
$$H_2(1,0) = 0.$$

Lemma 2 *For all positive integers* $n \geq 1$,

(2) $\quad H_{n+1}(p_1,p_2,...,p_n,0) = H_n(p_1,p_2,...,p_n).$

Proof In $H_n(p_1,p_2,...,p_n)$, we may assume that $p_n > 0$ because, if it is not so, then, by (b), we can make the nth value of the nth argument to be positive and then re–label the elements. Now, by (c),

$$H_{n+1}(p_1,p_2,...,p_n,0) = H_n(p_1,p_2,...,p_n) + p_n H_2(1,0).$$

Using Lemma 1, we have

$$H_2(1,0) = 0.$$

Hence, Lemma 2 follows.

Lemma 3 *For all positive integers* $n \geq 2$, $m \geq 2$, *so that* $n+m-1 \geq 3$, *we have*

(3)
$$\left[\begin{aligned} &H_{n+m-1}(p_1,p_2,\ldots p_{n-1},q_1,q_2,\ldots,q_m) \\ &= H_n(p_1,p_2,\ldots,p_n) + p_n\, H_m\Big(\frac{q_1}{p_n},\frac{q_2}{p_n},\ldots,\frac{q_m}{p_n}\Big) \end{aligned} \right.$$

with

(4)
$$p_n = q_1 + q_2 + \ldots + q_m > 0.$$

Proof For $m = 2$, (3) and (4) taken together reduce to condition (c). Thus, for $m = 2$, (3) holds by supposition. We prove Lemma 3 by induction on m. By Lemma 3, it is clear that zero probabilities do not contribute anything to the value of the functions H_n, $n = 1,2,\ldots$. Hence, it is enough to assume each $q_i > 0$, $i = 1,2,\ldots,m$. Then, obviously, $p_n > 0$.

Suppose there exists a value of m, say m_0, such that (3) holds for $m = m_0$ but for all $n \geq 2$. Then, we prove that (3) holds also for $m = m_0 + 1$ and for all positive integers $n \geq 2$. Now

$$H_{n+m_0}(p_1,p_2,\ldots,p_{n-1},q_1,q_2,\ldots,q_{m_0}+1)$$

$$= H_{n+1}(p_1,p_2,\ldots,p_{n-1},q_1,p^*) + p^*\, H_{m_0}\left[\frac{q_2}{p^*},\frac{q_3}{p^*},\ldots,\frac{q_{m_0}+1}{p^*}\right]$$

where
$$\not{p} = q_2 + q_3 + ... + q_{m_0+1}.$$

But, by (c),
$$H_{n+1}(p_1,p_2,...,p_{n-1},q_1,\not{p})$$

$$\begin{cases} = H_n(p_1,p_2,...,p_{n-1},q_1+\not{p}) \\ +(q_1+\not{p})H_2\left[\dfrac{q_1}{q_1+\not{p}},\dfrac{q_2}{q_1+\not{p}}\right] \end{cases}$$

Now,
$$q_1+\not{p} = q_1+q_2...+q_{m_0+1} = \sum_{j=1}^{m_0+1} q_j.$$

Hence,
$$H_{n+m_0}(p_1,p_2,...,p_{n-1},q_1,q_2,...,q_{m_0+1})$$

$$\begin{cases} = H_n(p_1,p_2,...,p_{n-1},q_1+\not{p}) \\ + (q_1+\not{p})H_2\left[\dfrac{q_1}{1+\not{p}},\dfrac{q_2}{q_1+\not{p}}\right] + (\not{p})H_{m_0}\left[\dfrac{q_2}{\not{p}},\dfrac{q_{m_0}}{\not{p}}\right] \end{cases}$$

Also,
$$H_{m_0+1}\left[\dfrac{q_1}{q_1+\not{p}}, \dfrac{q_{m_0}}{q_1+\not{p}}, \dfrac{q_{m_0+1}}{q_1+\not{p}}\right]$$

$$= H_2\left[\dfrac{q_1}{q_1+\not{p}},\dfrac{\not{p}}{q_1+\not{p}}\right] + \left[\dfrac{\not{p}}{q_1+\not{p}}\right] + H_{m_0}\left[\dfrac{q_2}{\not{p}},...,\dfrac{q_{m_0+1}}{\not{p}}\right]$$

Consequently, we get

$$H_{n+m_0}(p_1, p_2, \ldots, p_{m_0}+1, q_1, q_2, \ldots, q_{m_0}+1)$$

$$\begin{bmatrix} = H_n \left[p_1, p_2, \ldots, p_{n-1}, q_1 + p^* \right] \\ + (q_1 + p^*) \, H_{m_0+1} \left[\dfrac{q_1}{q_1 + p^*}, \ldots, \dfrac{q_{m_0}+1}{q + p^*} \right] \end{bmatrix}$$

This completes the proof of Lemma 3.

Lemma 4 *For all positive integers,* $n, m_1, m_2, \ldots, m_n$, *we have*

$$H_{m_1+m_2+\cdots+m_n}(q_{11}, q_{12}, \ldots, q_{1m_1}; \ldots; q_{n1}, q_{n2}, \ldots, q_{nm_n})$$

$$= H_n(p_1, p_2, \ldots, p_n) + \sum_{i=1}^{n} p_i \, H_{m_i} \left[\frac{q_{i1}}{p_i}, \frac{q_{i2}}{p_i}, \ldots, \frac{q_{im_i}}{p_i} \right]$$

where

$$p_i = q_{i1} + q_{i2} + \ldots + q_{im_i} > 0.$$

Proof Using Lemma 3, we have

(6) $H_{m_1+m_2+\cdots+m_n}(q_{11}, q_{12}, \ldots, q_{1m_1}; \ldots; q_{n1}, q_{n2}, \ldots, q_{nm_n})$

$$\begin{bmatrix} = H_{m_1+m_2+ \cdots +m_{n-1}+1}\big(q_{11}, \ldots, q_{1m_1}; \ldots; q_{(n-1)1}, q_{(n-1)(m_n-1)}; p_n\big) \\ + p_n \, H_{m_n} \left[\dfrac{q_{n1}}{p_n}, \dfrac{q_{n2}}{p_n}, \ldots, \dfrac{q_{nm_n}}{p_n} \right] \end{bmatrix}$$

Because of (b), we can shift p_n to extreme in the first term on the RHS of (6) and then continue the above sort of reduction.

Continuing this process of reduction n times, we finally obtain (5). This completes the proof of Lemma 4.

To proceed further, we introduce the notion

(7) $$f(n) = H_n(\frac{1}{n},\frac{1}{n},...,\frac{1}{n}), \; n = 1,2,3,...$$

where f is a real–valued function whose domain is N^+, the set of positive integers. Clearly, $f(1) = H_1(1)$. By Lemmas 2 and 1, $H_2(1,0) = H_1(1) = 0$. Thus, $f(1) = 0$. We now prove some Lemmas concerning f.

Lemma 5 *The mapping* $f: N^+ \to \mathbb{R}$ *defined by (7) possesses the following properties:*

(8) $$f(nm) = f(m) + f(n); \; m, \; n = 1,2,...$$

(9) $$\mu_n = \frac{f(n)}{n} \to 0 \; as \; n \to \infty.$$

(10) $$\lim_{n \to \infty} [f(n) - f(n-1)] = 0.$$

Proof Let us choose $m_1 = m_2 = ... = m_n = m$, and

$$q_{ij} = \frac{1}{mn}, \; i = 1,2,...,n; \; j = 1,2,...,m; \; m,n = 1,2,3,...$$

Then, Lemma 4 gives

$$H_{mn}(\frac{1}{mn},\frac{1}{mn},...,...\frac{1}{mn})$$

$$= H_n(\tfrac{1}{n},\tfrac{1}{n},...,\tfrac{1}{n}) + \sum_{i=1}^{n} \tfrac{1}{n} H_m(\tfrac{1}{m},\tfrac{1}{m},...,\tfrac{1}{m})$$

$$= H_n(\tfrac{1}{n},\tfrac{1}{n},...,\tfrac{1}{n}) + H_m(\tfrac{1}{m},\tfrac{1}{m},...,\tfrac{1}{m})$$

which, with the notation (7) reduces to (8) immediately. This proves (8).

By (c), we have

$$H_n(\tfrac{1}{n}, \tfrac{1}{n}, ...,\tfrac{1}{n})$$

$$= H_2(\tfrac{1}{n}, 1 - \tfrac{1}{n}) + (1 - \tfrac{1}{n}) H_{n-1}(\tfrac{1}{n-1}, \tfrac{1}{n-1},...,\tfrac{1}{n-1}),$$

so that

(11) $$f(n) = H_2(\tfrac{1}{n}, 1 - \tfrac{1}{n}) + (1 - \tfrac{1}{n}) f(n-1).$$

Using the notations $\eta_n = H_2(\tfrac{1}{n}, 1 - \tfrac{1}{n})$, $\tau_n = \dfrac{f(n)}{n}$, we get

(12) $$\mu_n = [\eta_n/ n] - [(n-1)^2/n^2] \mu_{n-1}$$

Also, from (11), we have

(13) $$n\,\eta_n = n\,f(n) - (n-1)\,f(n-1).$$

From (13), it follows that

$$f(n) = \sum_{k=1}^{n} k\, \eta_k$$

so that

(14)
$$\mu_n = [1/n^2] \sum_{k=1}^{n} k\, \eta_k = \frac{n+1}{2n} \frac{2}{n(n+1)} \sum_{k=1}^{n} k\, \eta_k,$$
$$= \frac{n+1}{2n} \left[\sum_{k=1}^{n} k\, \eta_k \Big/ \frac{n(n+1)}{2} \right]$$

The quantity $\sum_{k=1}^{n} k\, \eta_k \Big/ \frac{n(n+1)}{2}$ is simply the arithmetic mean of $\frac{n(n+1)}{2}$ terms

$$\eta_1, \eta_2, \eta_2, \eta_3, \eta_3, \eta_3, \ldots, \eta_n, \eta_n, \ldots \eta_n.$$

The limit of this sequence is the same as $\lim_{n \to \infty} \eta_n$. But, making use of (a),

$$\begin{aligned}
\lim_{n \to \infty} \eta_n \quad &= \lim_{n \to \infty} H_2(\tfrac{1}{n}, 1 - \tfrac{1}{n}) \\
&= H_2(\lim_{n \to \infty} \tfrac{1}{n}, \lim_{n \to \infty} 1 - \tfrac{1}{n}) = H(0,1) \\
&= H_2(\lim_{n \to \infty} \tfrac{1}{n}, \lim_{n \to \infty} 1 - \tfrac{1}{n}) = H(1,0) \\
&= 0
\end{aligned}$$

Hence, the above sequence also tends to zero. To proceed further, we make use of the following standard result from real analysis.

If a_n is a sequence of real numbers such that

$$\lim_{n \to \infty} a_n = a, \text{ then } \lim_{n \to \infty} \left[\sum_{i=1}^{n} a_i/n \right] = a.$$

Making use of this result, it follows that

$$\lim_{n \to \infty} \frac{2}{n(n+1)} \sum_{i=1}^{n} k \, \eta_k = 0.$$

Hence, from (14), it follows that

$$\lim_{n \to \infty} \mu_n = 0.$$

Thus (9) is proved. Now,

$$\lim_{n \to \infty} [f(n) - f(n-1)] = \lim_{n \to \infty} [\eta_n - \frac{1}{n} f(n-1)]$$

$$= \lim_{n \to \infty} \eta_n - \lim_{n \to \infty} (1 - \frac{1}{n}) \mu_n - 1 = 0 - 0 = 0$$

This proves (10).

Lemma 6 $f(n) = c \log n$, $n = 1, 2, \ldots$, *where c is an arbitrary constant.*

Proof Let us choose arbitrarily any positive integer $m > 1$ and define $g: N^+ \to \mathbb{R}$ as

$$(15) \qquad g(n) = f(n) - \frac{f(N) \log n}{\log N}$$

Then, it is easy to see that g satisfies the following:

$$(16) \qquad g(nm) = g(n) + g(m); \; n,m, = 1,2,3,...$$

$$(17) \qquad \lim_{n \to \infty} [g(n+1) - g(n)] = 0. \; \text{(by using (10))}$$

$$g(N) = 0.$$

Define G: $\{-1\} \cup \{0,1,2,...\} \to \mathbb{R}$ as

$$(18) \qquad \begin{cases} G(-1) = 0 \\ G(k) = \max_{N^k \le n < N^{k+1}} |g(n)|, \\ k = 0,1,2,... \end{cases}$$

If we put

$$(19) \qquad \begin{cases} \delta_k = \max_{N^k \le n < N^{k+1}} |g(n+1) - g(n)|, \\ k = 0,1,2,... \end{cases}$$

then, it is easy to see that

$$(20) \qquad \lim_{k \to \infty} \delta_k = 0.$$

Hence

(21)
$$\lim_{m \to \infty} \frac{1}{m} \sum_{k=1}^{m} \delta_k = 0$$

Now we prove that

(22)
$$\lim_{n \to \infty} \frac{g(n)}{\log n} = 0.$$

Let $n \in [N^k, N^{k+1})$. Then, by (18), we have $\frac{|g(n)|}{\log n} \leq \frac{G(k)}{k \log N}$.

Thus, in order to prove (22), it is enough to show that

(23)
$$\lim_{k \to \infty} \frac{G(k)}{k} = 0.$$

Now, let n be any positive integer. Choose k satisfying the inequalities $N^k \leq n < N^{k+1}$. Let $n' = N [\frac{n}{N}]$ where $[x]$ denotes the integral part of x i.e. the largest positive integer $\leq x$. Then $0 \leq n - n' < N$ and also n' is the greatest multiple of N. Now

$$g(n) = g(n-n'+n') = g(n') + g(n-n').$$

Hence

(24)
$$\begin{cases} |g(n)| \leq |g(n')| + |g(n-n')| \\ \leq |g(n')| + \sum_{\ell=n}^{n-1} |g(\ell+1) - g(\ell)| \\ \leq |g(n')| + N \delta_k. \end{cases}$$

Also

$$g(n') = g(N[\frac{n}{N}]) = g(N) + g(\frac{n}{N}) = g([\frac{n}{N}]).$$

Hence, using the inequalities $N^{k-1} \leq [\frac{n}{N}] < [\frac{n}{N}] N^k$, (24) gives

(25) $\qquad G(k) \leq G(k-1) + N \, \delta_k; \, k = 0,1,2,...$

Putting $k = 0,1,2,...,m$ and adding the inequalities so obtained, we get

$$\frac{G(m)}{m} \leq N \left[\frac{\delta_0 + \delta_1 + ... + \delta_m}{m} \right]$$

Let $m \to \infty$. Then, making use of (21), we immediately obtain (23). Now (15) gives

$$\frac{g(n)}{\log n} = \frac{f(n)}{\log n} - \frac{f(N)}{\log n}$$

Letting $n \to \infty$ and making use of (22), we arrive at

(26) $\qquad \lim_{n \to \infty} \frac{f(n)}{\log n} = \frac{f(N)}{\log N}$

Since $N < 1$ was chosen arbitrarily, therefore, the RHS of (26) does not depend upon N and hence it must be a constant which may be denoted by c. Consequently, we get $f(N) = c \log N$, $N > 1$. Also, $f(1) = 0$. Thus, $f(n) = c \log n$, $n = 1,2,3,...$ This proves Lemma 6.

Proof of the Theorem With these lemmas, we complete the proof of Theorem 1. It is enough to find the form of

$H_2(p,1-p)$ because by induction on n, the form of $H_n(p_1,p_2,...,p_n)$ can then be found out.

Let $p = \dfrac{r}{s}$, $r < s$, r and s being positive integers. Then, by Lemma 4, we have

$$f(s) = H_s(\tfrac{1}{s},\tfrac{1}{s},...,\tfrac{1}{s})$$

$$\begin{bmatrix} = H_2(\tfrac{r}{s},\ 1-\tfrac{r}{s}) + \tfrac{r}{s}\ H_r(\tfrac{1}{r},\tfrac{1}{r},...,\tfrac{1}{r}) \\ +\tfrac{s-r}{s}\ H_{s-r}(\tfrac{1}{s-r},\tfrac{1}{s-r},...,\tfrac{1}{s-r}) \end{bmatrix}$$

from which it follows that

(27)
$$\begin{bmatrix} H_2(p,1-p) \\ = f(s) - p\ f(r) - (1-p)\ f(s-r) \\ = c \log s - c\ p \log r - (1-p)\ c \log (s-r) \\ = c\ [p \log \tfrac{s}{r} + (1-p) \log \tfrac{s}{s-r}] \\ = c\ [-p \log p - (1-p) \log (1-p)]. \end{bmatrix}$$

Since $p \rightarrow H_2(p,1-p)$ is a continuous function of $p\ \epsilon\ [0,1]$ by (a), therefore, the above result also extends to all irrationals p and $p = 0,1$. This completes the proof of Theorem 1.

By this time, several axiomatic characterizations of the Shannon entropy are available in the literature. The proof of

Theorem 1 is the same as that given by Fadeev (1956) with the only modification that the proof of Lemma 6 is due to Rényi (1960).

From the above proof, it is obvious that up to (27), the condition (a) has not been used and all the conclusions obtained up to (27) make use of only the conditions (b) and (c).

If (c) is dropped, then one has to evolve a new system of axioms. Khinchin (1953) retained the conditions (a) and (b) but assumed additionally the Lemmas 2 and 4 and the fact that

$$H_n(p_1, p_2, ..., p_n) \leq H_n(\frac{1}{n}, \frac{1}{n}, ..., \frac{1}{n}) = f(n).$$

These assumptions imply that $n \to f(n)$ is a monotonically increasing function of n and the fact that f satisfies functional equation (8) from which it follows then that $f(1) = 0$ and $f(n) > 0$ for $n = 2, 3, ...$ These observations considerably simplify the proof of Lemma 6. Since (c) has been dropped, therefore, to determine the form of H_2 or H_n, a slightly different technique is needed. In the proof of Fadeev (1956), it is not possible to conclude that $n \to f(n)$ is a monotonic increasing function of n. However, (8) and (10) enable us to conclude that $f(n) = c \log n$ and hence there is no need to know the monotonic nature of

$$n \to f(n).$$

1.1.2 The Tverberg Characterization

Tverberg (1958) gave an axiomatic characterization of the Shannon entropy by weakening the condition of continuity on the mapping

$$p \to H_2 (p, 1-p), \; 0 \leq p \leq 1.$$

His theorem is as follows:

Theorem 1. *If* $H_n : \Delta_n \to \mathbb{R}$ *satisfies the condition* (c) *of Theorem 1 in 1.1.1 and further also the conditions*

(d) $p \to H_2 (p, 1-p)$ *is a real valued Lebesque integrable function of* $p \in [0,1]$

(e) H_2 *and* H_3 *are symmetric functions of their arguments.*

then H_n *is of the form:*

(A) $$H_n(p_1, p_2, ..., p_n) = - c \sum_{i=1}^{n} p_i \log_2 p_i$$

where c *is an arbitrary real constant.*

Proof By (1) of 1.1.1, for n = 3, we have

$$\left[\begin{array}{l} H_3(\alpha,\beta,\gamma) = H_2(\alpha,\beta,\gamma) + (\beta+\gamma) \, H_2(\frac{\beta}{\beta+\gamma},\frac{\gamma}{\beta+\gamma}), \\ \alpha \in [0,1), \; \beta \in [0,1), \; \alpha + \beta \in [0,1] \end{array} \right.$$

Obviously, using the symmetry of H_3 [condition (e)] we have

(1)
$$\left[\begin{array}{l} H_2(\alpha,\beta+\gamma) + (\beta+\gamma) \, H_2(\frac{\beta}{\beta+\gamma},\frac{\gamma}{\beta+\gamma}) \\ = H_2(\beta,\alpha+\gamma) + (\alpha+\gamma) \, H_2(\frac{\alpha}{\alpha+\gamma},\frac{\gamma}{\alpha+\gamma}) \end{array} \right.$$

Let us put

(2) $$h(p) = H_2(p,1-p), \; 0 \leq p \leq 1.$$

By the symmetry of H_2, we have $H_2(p,1-p) = H_2(1-p,p)$.
Hence

(3) $$h(p) = h(1-p), \; 0 \leq p \leq 1.$$

Consequently, (1) gives

(4)
$$\left[\begin{array}{l} h(\alpha) + (1-\alpha) \, h(\frac{\beta}{1-\alpha}) = h(\beta) + (1-\beta) \, h(\frac{\alpha}{1-\beta}) \\ \\ \alpha \in [0,1], \beta \in [0,1], \; \alpha + \beta \in [0,1]. \end{array} \right.$$

By condition (d), h is a Lebesque–integrable function of $p \in [0,1]$. Carrying out the integration with respect to $\beta \in [0,1-\alpha]$ and making the necessary change of variables, we obtain

(5)
$$\left[\begin{array}{l} (1-\alpha) \, h(\alpha) + (1-\alpha)^2 \int_0^1 h(t) \, dt \\[2mm] = \int_0^{1-\alpha} h(t) \, dt + \alpha^2 \int_\alpha^1 t^{-3} h(t) \, dt. \end{array} \right.$$

All the three terms in (5), involving integrals, determine continuous functions of $\alpha \in (0,1)$. Hence, h is also a continuous function of α for $\alpha \in (0,1)$. Also it can be inferred that h is a differentiable function of $\alpha \in (o,1)$. Differentiating (5) with respect to α, we get

$$\left[\begin{array}{l} (1-\alpha) \, h'(\alpha) - h(\alpha) - 2(1-\alpha) \int_0^1 h(t) \, dt \\[2mm] = h(1-\alpha) + 2\alpha \int_\alpha^1 t^{-3} h(t) \, dt - \alpha^{-1} h(\alpha) \end{array} \right.$$

which, with the aid of (3) reduces to

(6)
$$\left[\begin{array}{l} (1-\alpha) \, h'(\alpha) - 2(1-\alpha) \int_0^1 h(t) \, dt \\[2mm] = 2\alpha \int_\alpha^1 t^{-3} h(t) \, dt - \alpha^{-1} h(\alpha). \end{array} \right.$$

By the above reasoning, we can conclude that h' is differentiable so that $h''(\alpha)$ exists finitely. Differentiating (6) with respect to α and eliminating $\int_0^1 t^{-3} h(t)dt$, we get

$$h'(\alpha) = \frac{-2}{\alpha (1-\alpha)} \int_0^1 h(t) \, dt, \; \alpha \in (0,1)$$

from which it follows that

(7)
$$\begin{cases} h(\alpha) = c_2 \, \alpha + c_3 \\ - 2 \, [\alpha \log \alpha + (1-\alpha) \log (1-\alpha)] \int_0^1 h(t) \, dt \end{cases}$$

In the light of (3), it follows that $c_2 = 0$ and then if we integrate with respect to α between the limits 0 and 1, we get $c_3 = 0$ so that finally setting $2 \int_0^1 h(t)dt = c$, we get

(8)
$$h(\alpha) = c \, [-\alpha \log \alpha - (1-\alpha) \log (1-\alpha)], \; \alpha \in (0,1)$$

Also (3) gives
$$h(0) = h(1)$$

But if we put $\beta = 1-\alpha$ in (4), we get $h(1) = 0$. Thus

(9)
$$h(0) = h(1) = 0$$

From (8) and (9), it follows that

(10)
$$\begin{cases} H_2(\alpha,1-\alpha) = h(\alpha) \\ = c \, [-\alpha \log \alpha - (1-\alpha) \log (1-\alpha)], \; \alpha \in [0,1] \end{cases}$$

Thus, we have found out the form of H_2. The form of H_n may be found out by induction.

1.1.3 The Lee Characterization

Lee (1964) gave an axiomatic characterization of the Shannon entropy. He proved the following theorem:

Theorem 1: *If* $H_n : \Delta_n \to \mathbb{R}$ *satisfies the conditions* (c) *of* 1.1.1, *and* (e) *of* 1.1.2 *and the condition*

(f) $\qquad p \to H_2(p, 1-p)$ *is a finite real–valued Lebesque*

measurable function defined on $(0,1)$, *then* H_n *is of the form*

(A) $\qquad H_n(p_1, p_2, ..., p_n) = -c \sum_{i=1}^{n} p_i \log_2 p_i$

where c *is an arbitrary real constant.*

Before we prove the above theorem, we would like to compare it with Theorem 1 of 1.1.2 [Tverberg (1958)]. It is clear that conditions (c) and (e) are common to Theorem 1 of 1.1.2 and Theorem 1 above and hence one can easily arrive at the functional equation (4) of 1.1.2 and then our problem simply reduces to finding the Lebesque measurable solutions of

(4) of 1.1.2 Our discussion is based on several Lemmas as follows:

Lemma 1 *Let J ⊂ (0,1) be a Lebesque−measurable set of measure c > 0. Then*

$$K_y = \{\frac{x}{1-(1-x)y} : x \in J\}$$

is a Lebesque−measurable set for each y ∈ [a,b] ⊂ (0,1) and $\mu(K_y) > (1-b)$ c where $\mu(.)$ denotes the Lebesque measure of the set under consideration.

Proof In the proof of this Lemma, we need the following result from Zaanen (1958): Let μ denote Lebesque measure in $\mathbb{R}$ and $\phi: \mathbb{R} \to \mathbb{R}$ be a continuously differentiable increasing function with a strictly positive derivative which maps an open interval I into an open interval $\phi(I)$. Then ϕ maps every Lebesque−measurable subset J of I to a Lebesque−measurable subset $\phi(J)$ of $\phi(I)$ and

(1) $$\mu(\phi(J)) = \int_J \phi'(t)dt.$$

Let us choose $\phi_y(x) = \frac{x}{1-(1-x)y}$, x ∈ (0,1), y ∈ [a,b]. For each fixed y ∈ [a,b], it can be easily verified that ϕ is a continuously differentiable strictly increasing function with a strictly positive derivative and maps the open interval (0,1) onto an open interval $\phi(I)$. Hence it maps every Lebesque−measurable subset $J \subset (0,1)$ to a Lebesque–measurable subset $\phi(J)$ of $\phi[(0,1)]$. Let us set

$$J = (r,s) \subset (0,1).$$

Then, (1) gives

$$\mu(\phi(J)) = \mu(K_y) = \int_J \phi'(x)dx = [\phi_y(x)]_r^s$$

$$= [\frac{x}{1-(1-x)y}]_r^s = [\frac{s}{1-(1-s)y} - \frac{r}{1-(1-r)y}]$$

$$= \frac{(s-r)}{[1-(1-s)y]} \frac{(1-y)}{[1-(1-r)y]} = \frac{c(1-y)}{[1-(1-s)y]} \frac{}{[1-(1-r)y]}$$

Since $y \in [a,b]$, therefore, $y \le b \to 1-y \ge 1-b$. Also

$$\frac{1}{1-(1-s)y} \quad \text{and} \quad \frac{1}{1-(1-r)y}$$

are both greater than unity. Hence, $\mu(K_y) > c(1-b)$ which proves the Lemma.

Lemma 2   *Let $E \subset [0,1]$ be a Lebesque–measurable set symmetrical about the point $\frac{1}{2}$ and of positive measure. Then, there exists $k \ge 2$, $[a,b] \subset (0,1)$, $a < b$, $c > 0$ such that any $y \in [a,b]$ can be expressed in the form $y = \frac{\gamma}{1-y}$ with γ and η both in the set $E \cap (\frac{1}{k}, 1 - \frac{1}{k})$ for a Lebesque–measurable set of distinct values of η and of measure at least c.*

Proof Let us choose $k \geq 2$ such that $G = E \cap (\frac{1}{k}, 1 - \frac{1}{k})$ has positive measure. Let χ_G denote the characteristic function of G. Since G is measurable, therefore, χ_G is also a Lebesque—measurable function so that $\chi_G \in L^1_\mu$. Since the continuous functions are dense in L^1_μ, therefore, given any $\epsilon > 0$, there exists a continuous function f such that $\|\chi_G - f\|_1 < \epsilon/2$. Now, let $y \in [a,b]$. Then

$$\|\chi_G(yx) - \chi_G(x)\|_1$$

$$= \|\chi_G(yx) - f(yx) + f(yx) - f(x) + f(x) - \chi_G(x)\|_1$$

$$\leq \|\chi_G(yx) - f(yx)\|_1 + \|f(yx - f(x)\|_1 + \|f(x) - \chi_G(x)\|_1.$$

Since $x \in (0,1)$, $y \in [a,b] \subset (0,1)$ imply $xy \in (0,1)$, therefore

$$\|\chi_G(yx) - \chi_G(x)\|_1 \leq \|f(y) - f(x)\|_1 + \epsilon.$$

Since f is continuous on $[0,1]$, therefore, it is also uniformly continuous on $[0,1]$. Hence, as a consequence of uniform continuity, we have

$$\lim_{y \uparrow 1} \int_0^1 |f(yx) - f(x)| \, \mu(dx) = 0$$

which means

$$\lim_{y \uparrow 1} \|f(yx) - f(x)\|_1 = 0.$$

Consequently,

$$\lim \|\chi_G(yx) - \chi_G(x)\|_1 = 0.$$

Then,

$$\lim \mu\{\eta: \eta \in G, (1-\eta)y \in G\}$$

$$= \lim \mu\{x: x \in G, xy \in G\}$$

$$= \lim \int \chi_G(xy) \, \mu(dx)$$

$$= \mu(G) > 0.$$

Upon setting $(1-\eta)y = \gamma$, $\frac{1}{2} \mu(G) = c$, and choosing a and b such that for each $y \in [a,b]$, $(1-\eta) y \in G$, $y \in G$, the Lemma is proved.

Lemma 3 *Every measurable solution of (4) of 1.1.2 satisfying the symmetry condition (3) of 1.1.2 is bounded on some interval.*

Proof Since h, satisfying (4) of · 1.1.2 is a Lebesque—measurable function, therefore, for each positive integer n, the set

$$E_n = \{\xi: 0 < \xi < 1, |h(\xi)| > n\}$$

is measurable and of measure ≤ 1. Also, $\lim E_n = \phi$. Hence, there exists a positive integer N such that when

$$E = \{\xi: 0 < \xi < 1, \; |h(\xi)| \leq N\},$$

then $\mu((E) \geq \frac{1}{2}$. Since $h(\xi) = h(1-\xi)$, therefore, E is symmetric about $\frac{1}{2}$. Define

$$G = E \cap (\tfrac{1}{k}, 1 - \tfrac{1}{k})$$

and choose k, a, b and c as specified in Lemma 2. Let $y \; \epsilon \; [a,b]$ $\subset (0,1)$. Then, we may write $y = \frac{\gamma}{1-\eta}$ in several ways with γ and η belonging to G. Since , $0 < a \leq y \leq e < 1$, therefore,

$$0 < \tfrac{\gamma}{1-\eta} < 1 \; \Rightarrow \; 0 < \eta < 1-\gamma \; \Rightarrow \; 0 < \tfrac{\eta}{1-\gamma} < 1$$

and hence, by Lemma 1 the set K_y of all positive value of the form $\frac{\eta}{1-(1-\eta)y}$ covers a Lebesque—measurable set with measure greater than $(1-b)c$. Consequently, there must exist a positive integer $M \geq N$ such that the set

$$F = \{\xi: 0 < \xi < 1, \; |h(\xi)| > M\}$$

has its measure $\mu(F) < \frac{1}{2} c \, (1-b)$. Then for every $y \; \epsilon \; [a,b]$, there exists at least one representation of the form $y = \frac{\gamma}{1-\eta}$ where γ and η belonging to G and $\frac{\eta}{1-\gamma} \notin F$. Now, using the symmetry of h, we have

$$|h(y)| = |h(\tfrac{\gamma}{1-\eta})|$$

$$= (1-\eta)^{-1} \, | h(\gamma) + (1-\gamma) \, h(\tfrac{\eta}{1-\gamma}) - h\,(\eta) |$$

$$\leq (1-\eta)^{-1} \{ |h(\gamma)| + |h(\tfrac{\eta}{1-\gamma})| + |h(\eta)| \}$$

$$< 3kM$$

Thus, h is bounded. This proves Lemma 3.

Lemma 4 *Every measurable solution of* (4) *of* 1.1.2 *satisfying the condition* (3) *of* 1.1.2, *is bounded on every compact subset of* $(0,1)$.

Proof Let $\Lambda = \{\lambda \colon \lambda > 0$ and $h\,(\alpha) - \lambda h\,(\alpha/\lambda)$ be bounded as $\alpha{\downarrow}0\}$ Obviously, $1 \in \Lambda$. Now, let $0 < \lambda_1 \in \Lambda$ and $0 < \lambda_2 \in \Lambda$. Then,

$$h\,(\alpha) - \lambda_1 \, h(\tfrac{\alpha}{\lambda_1}) \quad \text{and} \quad h(\alpha) - \lambda_2 \, h(\tfrac{\alpha}{\lambda_2})$$

are bounded as $\alpha \downarrow 0$. Then,

$$|h(\alpha) - \lambda_1 \lambda_2 \, h(\tfrac{\alpha}{\lambda_1\lambda_2})|$$

$$\leq |h\,(\alpha) - \lambda_1 \, h(\tfrac{\alpha}{\lambda_1})| + \lambda_1 \, |h(\tfrac{\alpha}{\lambda_1}) - \lambda_2 \, h(\tfrac{\alpha}{\lambda_1\lambda_2})|$$

from which it follows that

$$h\,(\alpha) - \lambda_1 \lambda_2 \, h(\tfrac{\alpha}{\lambda_1\lambda_2}) \text{ is bounded as } \alpha \downarrow 0.$$

Hence, $\lambda_1 \lambda_2 \in \Lambda$. Finally, let $\lambda \in \Lambda$. Then, one can easily see that $(1/\lambda) \in \Lambda$. With these observations, we conclude that Λ is a multiplicative group. Note that associative law is trivially satisfied.

Now, by Lemma 3, there exists some open interval $J \subset (0,1)$ on which h is bounded. If $1-\lambda \in J$, then by 1.1.2 (4)

$$(2) \quad h(\alpha) - \lambda\, h(\tfrac{\alpha}{\lambda}) = h(1-\lambda) - (1-\alpha)\, h(\tfrac{1-\lambda}{1-\lambda}),\ 0 < \alpha < \lambda < 1,$$

so that $\lambda \in \Lambda$. Thus $1-\lambda \in J$ $\lambda \in \Lambda$. Consequently, Λ covers a measurable set of positive measure and hence it must be the whole of $(0,\infty)$ i.e., $\Lambda = (0,\infty)$. Making use of (e) and the equation (2), it follows that $t = 1-\lambda \in (0,1)$ lies in an open interval on which h is bounded. Thus, h is bounded on each compact subset of $(0,1)$.

Proof of the Theorem   Integration of 1.1.2 (4) with respect to $\beta \in [\lambda,\mu]$ gives

$$(\mu-\lambda)\, h(\alpha) \quad \left[\begin{aligned} &= \int_\lambda^\mu h(\gamma)d\gamma \\[2mm] &\quad + \alpha^2 \int_{\alpha/\{1-\lambda\}}^{\alpha/\{1-\mu\}} \gamma^3\, h(\gamma)\, d\gamma \\[2mm] &\quad - (1-\alpha)^2 \int_{\lambda/\{1-\alpha\}}^{\mu/\{1-\alpha\}} h(\gamma)d\gamma, \\[2mm] &0 < \alpha < \alpha + \lambda \leq \alpha + \mu < 1. \end{aligned}\right.$$

as in Theorem 1 of 1 1.2, we conclude that h is differentiable at every interior point of the unit interval. By condition (c)

$$H_3(\alpha,\beta,\gamma)$$

$$= H_2(\alpha+\beta,\gamma) + (\alpha \neq \beta) \, H_2\left[\frac{\alpha}{\alpha+\beta'}, \frac{\beta}{\alpha+\beta}\right]$$

$$= H_2(\alpha+\beta, 1-(\alpha+\beta)) + (\alpha+\beta) \, H_2\left[\frac{\alpha}{\alpha+\beta}, 1 - \frac{\alpha}{\alpha+\beta}\right]$$

$$= h(\alpha+\beta) + (\alpha+\beta) \, h\left[\frac{\alpha}{\alpha+\beta}\right].$$

Thus, we have

$$(3) \qquad h(\beta) + (1-\beta) \, h\left[\frac{\alpha}{1-\beta}\right] = h(\alpha+\beta) + (\alpha+\beta) \, h\left[\frac{\alpha}{\alpha+\beta}\right].$$

Since h is differentiable in (0,1), differentiating (3) with respect to α we get

$$(4) \qquad h'(\alpha+\beta)+h\left[\frac{\alpha}{\alpha+\beta}\right]+\left[\frac{\beta}{\alpha+\beta}\right]h'\left[\frac{\alpha}{\alpha+\beta}\right] = h'\left[\frac{\alpha}{1-\beta}\right]$$

Also, we have

$$(5) \qquad h(\alpha)+(1-\alpha)h\left[\frac{\beta}{1-\alpha}\right]-\left[\frac{\alpha}{\alpha+\beta}\right]h'\left[\frac{\alpha}{\alpha+\beta}\right] = h'\left[\frac{\beta}{1-\alpha}\right].$$

Differentiating with respect to β, we get

(6)
$$\left[h'(\alpha+\beta) + h\left[\frac{\alpha}{\alpha+\beta}\right] - \left[\frac{\alpha}{\alpha+\beta}\right] h'\left[\frac{\alpha}{\alpha+\beta}\right] \right.$$

$$\left. = h'\left[\frac{\beta}{1-\alpha}\right].\right.$$

From (5) and (6), we get

(7)
$$h'\left[\frac{\alpha}{\alpha+\beta}\right] = h'\left[\frac{\alpha}{1-\beta}\right] - h'\left[\frac{\beta}{1-\alpha}\right].$$

Setting $h'(t) = E\left[\frac{t}{1-t}\right]$, (7) becomes

(8)
$$E\left[\frac{\alpha}{\beta}\right] = E\left[\frac{\alpha}{1-\alpha-\beta}\right] - E\left[\frac{\beta}{1-\alpha-\beta}\right].$$

Putting

$$\alpha = \frac{uv}{1+v+uv}, \qquad \beta = \frac{v}{1+v+uv}$$

from which, of course, we get $u = \frac{\alpha}{\beta}$, $v = \frac{\beta}{1-\alpha-\beta}$. Then (8) reduces to

(9)
$$E(uv) = E(u) + E(v), v \in (0,\infty)$$

Since h' is also differentiable, therefore, it is continuous also. The continuous solutions of (9) are of the form $E(u) = c \log u$ where c is a constant. Hence

(10)
$$h'(t) = c \log t - c \log (1-t)$$

Integrating (10) with respect to t from $\frac{1}{2}$ to t, $t \in (0,1)$, we get

$$h(t) = -c\,t\,\log t - c\,(1-t)\,\log\,(1-t),\ t \in (0,1)$$

The rest of the arguments are the same as in Theorem 1 of 1.1.2.

1.1.4 Properties of the Shannon Entropy

In all the characterization theorems concerning $H_n: \Delta_n \to \mathbb{R}$, $n = 1,2,\ldots$ we have not assumed the normalization condition

(1)   (g) $H_2(\tfrac{1}{2},\tfrac{1}{2}) = 1$

If (g) is assumed, then we have

(2)
$$\begin{cases} H_n(p_1,p_2,\ldots,p_n) = \displaystyle\sum_{i=1}^{n} p_i \log_2 p_i, \\[2mm] (p_1,p_2,\ldots,p_n) \in \Delta_n,\ n = 1,2,\ldots \end{cases}$$

where

(3) $0 \log_2 0 = \displaystyle\lim_{x \to 0^+} x \log_2 x = 0$

The quantity (2) is called the Shannon entropy. In this section, our object is to give various algebraic and analytic properties of (2) and prove some related theorems.

P_1 For all positive integers n, the Shannon Entropy $H_n: \Delta_n \rightarrow \mathbb{R}$, n = 1,2,... is a continuous function of its arguments.

P_2 For all positive integers $n \geq 2$, $H_n: \Delta_n \rightarrow \mathbb{R}$, n = 1,2,..., is a symmetric function of its arguments.

P_3 For all positive integers $n \geq 1,2,...$

$$\begin{cases} H_{n+1}(p_1,p_2,...,p_n,0) = H_n(p_1,p_2,...,p_n) \\ \\ (p_1,p_2,...,p_n) \in \Delta_n; \ (p_1,p_2,...,p_n,0) \in \Delta_{n+1}. \end{cases}$$

P_4 $H_2(\tfrac{1}{2},\tfrac{1}{2}) = 1.$

P_5 $H_2(1,0) = H_2(0,1) = 0.$

P_6 H_n is additive for all positive integers n, that is, H_n satisfies

$$H_{nm}(p_1q_1,p_1q_2,...,p_1q_m;...;p_nq_1,p_nq_2,...,p_nq_m)$$

$$\begin{cases} = H_n(p_1,p_2,...,p_n) + H_m(q_1,q_2,...,q_m), \\ \\ (p_1,..,p_n) \in \Delta_n, \ (q_1,..,q_m) \in \Delta_m; \ m,n = 1,2,3,... \end{cases}$$

P_7 For all positive integers $n \geq 3$,

(4)
$$\begin{bmatrix} H_{n+1}(p_1,p_2,..,p_{n-2},q_1,q_2) \\[2mm] = H_n(p_1,p_2,..,p_{n-2},q_1+q_2)+(q_1+q_2)H_2\left[\dfrac{q_1}{q_1+q_2},\dfrac{q_2}{q_1+q_2}\right], \\[2mm] q_1+q_2 > 0,\ p_1+p_2+...+p_{n-2}+\ q_1+q_2 = 1. \end{bmatrix}$$

P_8 H_n is strongly additive i.e.,

(5)
$$\begin{bmatrix} H_{nm}(r_{11},r_{12},..,r_{1m};\ r_{21},r_{22},..,r_{2m};...;r_{n1},r_{n2},..,r_{mn}) \\[2mm] = H_n(p_1,p_2,..,p_n) + \sum_{i=1}^{n} p_i\ H_m(r_{1/i},r_{2/i},..,r_{m/i}) \end{bmatrix}$$

P_9 $H_n : \Delta_n \to \mathbb{R},\ n = 1,2,...$ achieves its maximum value if and only if $p_1 = p_2 ... = p_n = \frac{1}{n}$ i.e.,

(6) $H_n(p_1,p_2,..,p_n) \leq \log_2 n$

with equality if and only if $p_i = \frac{1}{n},\ i = 1,2,...n.$

P_{10} $H_n : \Delta_n \to \mathbb{R}$ is sub additive in the sense that

(7)
$$\begin{bmatrix} H_{nm}(r_{11},r_{12},..,r_{1m};\ r_{21},r_{22},..,r_{2m};...;r_{n1},..,r_{nm}) \\[2mm] \leq H_m\left[\sum_{i=1}^{n} r_{i1},\ \sum_{i=1}^{n} r_{i2},...,\ \sum_{i=1}^{n} r_{im}\right] \\[2mm] + H_n\left[\sum_{j=1}^{m} r_{1j},\ \sum_{j=1}^{m} r_{2j},...,\ \sum_{j=1}^{m} r_{nj}\right] \end{bmatrix}$$

with equality if and only if

$$(8) \qquad r_{ij} = \left[\sum_{i=1}^{n} r_{ij}, \sum_{i=1}^{n} r_{ij} \right]; i = 1,..,n; j = 1,..,m.$$

The proof of properties P_1 to P_8 are quite simple and we omit them. Below, we give the proofs of P_9 and P_{10}.

Proof of P_9 For any two probability distributions $(p_1,p_2,...,p_n) \in \Delta_n$ and $(q_1,q_2,...,q_n) \in \Delta_n$, $n = 1,2,3,...$

$$(9) \qquad -\sum_{i=1}^{n} p_i \log_2 p_i \le -\sum_{i=1}^{n} p_i \log_2 q_i$$

with equality iff

$$(10) \qquad p_i = q_i, i = 1,2,...,n.$$

Indeed, for $n = 1$, the proof is trivial. If, for some value of i, $q_i = 0$ but the corresponding $p_i \ne 0$, even then (9) holds trivially because $-\log x \to +\infty$ as $x \to 0^+$. Also, if $p_i = 0$ for some value or values of i irrespective of whether the corresponding $q_i = 0$ or not, then $p_i \log p_i = p_i \log q_i = 0$. Let us exclude all those indices i for which $p_i = 0$ but $q_i \ne 0$. Then $\sum_i q_i \le \sum_i p_i$ where now i varies only over those values of i for which $p_i = 0$ and $q_i \ne 0$. Since $\log_e x \le (x-1)$, it follows that $\log_2 x \le (x-1) \log_2 e$ with equality if and only if $x = 1$, and thus

(11) $\sum_i p_i \log \frac{q_i}{p_i} \leq \left(\sum_i q_i - \sum_i p_i \right) \log_2 e \leq 0$

where i varies over those indices for which $p_i \neq 0$, $q_i = 0$. Using the fact that $0 \log_2 q = 0$, $0 \leq q \leq 1$, the inequality (12) holds for all $i = 1,2,...,n$ and thus (9) is proved. The fact that equality holds in (9) is a simple consequence of the fact that, in (11), equality holds if and only if $p_i = q_i$ for all those indices i with $p_i \neq 0$, $q_i \neq 0$. Then $\sum_i p_i = \sum_i q_i$, i varying over those indices where $p_i \neq 0$, $q_i \neq 0$. But, then $\sum p_i = \sum q_i = 1$ because i varies over all those indices for which $p_i \neq 0$, $q_i \neq 0$. Hence if there is an index i for which $p_i \neq 0$, then the corresponding q_i must also equal zero and conversely. Hence, equality in (9) holds if and only if (10) holds

Proof of P_{10} In (9), let us choose the probability distribution

$$\left(r_{11}, r_{12}, ..., r_{1m};\ r_{21}, r_{22}, ..., r_{2m};\ ...;\ r_{n1}, r_{n2}, ..., r_{mn} \right)$$

and

$$\left(p_1 q_1, .., p_1 p_m;\ p_2 q_1, p_2 q_2, .., p_2 q_m; ...;\ p_n q_1, p_n q_2, .., p_n q_m \right).$$

Then (9) gives

$$-\sum_{i=1}^{n} \sum_{j=1}^{m} r_{ij} \log r_{ij} \leq -\sum_{i=1}^{n} \sum_{j=1}^{m} r_{ij} \log p_i q_j$$

which gives (7) on simplification.

Property P_{10} can be interpreted as follows: The average amount of information obtained from the simultaneous performance of two experiments cannot exceed the sum of the average amounts of information given individually by the two experiments.

1.2 THE RENYI ENTROPY

Rényi (1960) introduced another measure of entropy, the so—called entropy of positive α—order or, as it is now known, the Rényi entropy of order $\alpha>0$ or, simply, the Rényi entropy. Here we shall embark upon a study of the Rényi entropy.

Of the early axiomatic characterizations of the Shannon entropy, the one which has got wide attention of researchers in information theory is that of Fadeev (1956) which is Theorem 1 of 1.1.1. If we assume the normalization condition

(1) $H_2(\tfrac{1}{2},\tfrac{1}{2},) = 1,$

then, Theorem 1 of 1.1.1 gives

(2)
$$\begin{cases} H_n(p_1,p_2,...,p_n) = -\sum_{k=1}^{n} p_k \log p_k, \\ (p_1,p_2,...,p_n) \in \Delta_n, \ n = 1,2,... \end{cases}$$

where

(3) $0 \log 0 = 0.$

As mentioned in Theorem 1 of 1.1.1, the condition (c) there plays a crucial role in this theorem. From Lemma 4 of 1.1.1, it is clear that H_n is additive in the sense that

(4)
$$\begin{cases} H_{nm}(p_1q_1,..,p_nq_1;p_1q_2,..,p_nq_2;..;p_1q_m,..,p_nq_m) \\ = H_n(p_1,p_2,...,p_n) + H_m(q_1,q_2,...,q_m), \\ (p_1,p_2,...,p_n) \in \Delta_n, \ (q_1,q_2,...,q_m) \in \Delta_m. \end{cases}$$

Thus, each $H_n: \Delta_n \to \mathbb{R}$ satisfying (b) and (c) of 1.1.1 is additive in the sense of (4). However, if each function $H_n: \Delta_n \to \mathbb{R}$, $n = 1,2,...$ is a symmetric function of its arguments for all positive integers n and m, then it need not satisfy (4) of 1.1.1 for all $n \geq 3$. In this sense, disregarding 1.1.1 (b) it is obvious that 1.1.1 (c) is much stronger than (4) and hence it cannot be replaced by (4). In fact, as pointed out by Rényi (1960), there are many other quantities in addition to (2), which satisfy (a), (b) of

1.1.1, (4) and (1). For example all the quantities (the Rényi entropies).

(5)
$$\left[\begin{array}{l} {}^{\alpha}H_n(p_1,p_2,...,p_n) = (1-\alpha)^{-1} \log (\sum_{k=1}^{n} p_k{}^{\alpha}), \\ \alpha > 0, (p_1,p_2,...,p_n) \, \epsilon \, \Delta_n, \, n = 1,2,... \end{array} \right.$$

satisfy (a), (b) of 1.1.1, (4) and (1). Note that (5) does not satisfy (c) of 1.1.1. Also,

$$\lim_{\alpha \to 1} {}^{\alpha}H_n(p_1,p_2,...,p_n)$$
$$= -\sum_{k=1}^{n} p_k \log p_k = H_n(p_1,p_2,...,p_n)$$

so that the Shannon entropy may be regarded as the Rényi entropy of order one. To discuss some characterizations of (5) is our main object here. The characterization of (5) becomes much easier if we make use of the concept of generalized probability distribution described earlier.

1.2.1 The Rényi Characterization

In this section, we shall discuss the axiomatic characterization of ${}^{\alpha}H_n$ due to Rényi (1960). We prove the following characterization theorem for generalized probability distributions with positive elements.

Theorem 1. *Let $K_n : \Delta_n \to \mathbb{R}$ be a sequence of functions possessing the following properties:*

(a*) K_1 *is a continuous function of* $p \in (0,1]$.

(b*) $\begin{cases} K_{n+1}(p_1,p_2,..,p_n,0) = K_n(p_1,p_2,..,p_n), \\[2ex] p_i \geq 0,\, i = 1,2,...,n,\, 0 < \sum\limits_{i=1}^{n} p_i \leq 1. \end{cases}$

(c*) $K_1\left(\tfrac{1}{2}\right) = 1$.

(d*)   *For all positive integers* n

$\begin{cases} K_n(p_1 q, p_2 q,..,p_n q) = K_n(p_1,p_2,..,p_n) + K_1(q), \\[2ex] q \in (0,1],\, p_i > 0,\, i = 1,2,...,n,\, \sum\limits_{i=1}^{n} p_i \leq 1, \end{cases}$

(e*)   *There exists a strictly monotonic and continuous function* $y = g(x)$ *defined for all real* x *such that for any generalized probability distribution* $(p_1,p_2,..,p_n)$ *with positive elements,*

$$\begin{cases} K_n(p_1,p_2,..,p_n) = g^{-1}\left[\dfrac{\sum\limits_{i=1}^{n} p_i K_1(p_i)}{\sum\limits_{i=1}^{n} p_i} \right], \\[4ex] p_i > 0,\, i = 1,2,...,n;\, \sum\limits_{i=1}^{n} p_i \leq 1. \end{cases}$$

where g^{-1} *denotes the inverse function of* g.

Then g *is necessarily either a linear or an exponential function. In the first case, that is, when* g *is linear,* $K_n = H_n$ *where*

$$(6) \qquad H_n(p_1, p_2, .., p_n) = -\left[\sum_{k=1}^{n} p_k \log p_k\right] / \left[\sum_{k=1}^{n} p_k\right]$$

In the second case, that is, when g *is exponential,* $K_n = {}^{\alpha}H_n$
where

$$(7) \qquad H_n(p_1, p_2, .., p_n)$$

$$\left[= (1-\alpha)^{-1} \log_2 \left[\sum_{k=1}^{n} p_k / \sum_{k=1}^{n} p_k\right],\right.$$

$$\left. \alpha > 0, \ \alpha \neq 1, \ (p_1, p_2, ..., p_n) \in \Delta'.\right.$$

Proof For $n = 1$, (d*) gives

$$(8) \qquad K_1(pq) = K_1(p) + K_1(q), \ p \in (0,1], \ q \in (0,1]$$

By (a*), K_1 is a continuous function of $p \in (0,1]$. Hence, the continuous solutions of (8) are of the form

$$K_1(p) = \lambda \log_2 p$$

where λ is an arbitrary constant. By (c*), $K_1\left(\frac{1}{2}\right) = 1$. Hence $\lambda = -1$ so that

$$(9) \qquad K_1(p) = \log_2\left(\frac{1}{2}\right), \ p \in (0,1].$$

Let $(p_1, p_2, .., p_n)$ be any generalized probability distribution. Then , by (e*), we get

$$(10) \qquad K_n(p_1,p_2,..,p_n) = g^{-1}\left[\sum_{i=1}^{n} p_i\, g(\log_2 \frac{1}{p_i})\, /\, \sum_{i=1}^{m} p_i\right]$$

Then by (d*), we get

$$(11) \qquad \left[g^{-1}\left[\sum_{i=1}^{m} p_i\, g(\log_2 \frac{1}{p_i} + \log \frac{1}{q})\, /\, \sum_{i=1}^{m} p_i\right] \right.$$

$$\left. = g^{-1}\left[\sum_{i=1}^{m} p_i\, g(\log_2 \frac{1}{p_i})\, /\, \sum_{i=1}^{m} p_i\right] + \log_2 \frac{1}{q}. \right.$$

Let us write

$$(12) \qquad \left[w_i = p_i\, /\, \sum_{k=1}^{n} p_k;\ x_i = \log_2 \frac{1}{p_i}\ \text{and}\ y = \log_2 \frac{1}{q} \right.$$

$$\left. i = 1,2,...,n. \right.$$

Since all p_i's and q are positive, therefore $w_i > 0$, $x_i \geq 0$, $y \geq 0$, $i = 1,2,...,n$. For the sake of convenience, we choose $q \in (0,1)$ so that $y > 0$. Then (12) reduces to

$$(13) \qquad g^{-1}\left[\sum_{i=1}^{n} w_i\, g(x_i+y)\right] = g^{-1}\left[\sum_{i=1}^{n} w_i\, g(x_i) + y\right]$$

By substituting

$$(14) \qquad g_y(x) = g(x+y),$$

we may write (13) as

$$(15) \qquad g_y^{-1}\left[\sum_{i=1}^{n} w_i\, g_y(x_i)\right] = g^{-1}\left[\sum_{i=1}^{n} w_i\, g(x_i)\right]$$

In other words, the functions g and g_y generate the same mean value. Our object is to find the relationship between g and g_y. Of course, it is trivially seen that g_y is also strictly monotonic and continuous. In order to find the relationship, we need the following lemmas [Hardy et al, (1952)]

Lemma 1 *In order that*

$$\begin{bmatrix} \Psi^{-1}\left[\sum_{i=1}^{n} q_i\, \Psi(a_i)\right] = \phi^{-1}\left[\sum_{i=1}^{n} q_i\, \phi(a_i)\right] \\ q_i > 0,\ \sum_{i=1}^{n} q_i = 1,\ a_i \geq 0,\ i = 1,2,...,n \end{bmatrix}$$

it is necessary and sufficient that

$$\phi = \alpha\, \Psi + \beta$$

where α and β are constants and $\alpha \neq 0$.

Making use of this Lemma, (15) gives

$$(16) \qquad g_y(x) = a(y)\, g(x) + b(y)$$

where $a(y) \neq 0$ and by b(y) are constants. From (14) and (16), it follows that

(17) $g(x+y) = a(y) g(x) + b(y).$

Without any loss of generality, we may assume that $g(0) = 0$. This gives $b(y) = g(y)$ so that

(18) $g(x+y) = a(y) g(y) + g(y).$

Equation (18) holds for all x and y. Interchanging the role of x and y, we thus obtain

(19) $g(x+y) = a(x) g(y) + g(x).$

From (18) and (19). we get

(20) $a(y) g(x) + g(y) = a(x) g(y) + g(x).$

Now, by assumption, g is a strictly monotonic and continuous function with $g(0) = 0$. Hence, if we restrict to $x \neq 0$, $y \neq 0$, then, obviously we must have

(21) $\dfrac{a(y)-1}{g(y)} = \dfrac{a(x)-1}{g(x)}$, $x \neq 0, y \neq 0.$

Consequently, we have

(22) $\begin{cases} a(x)-1 = k\, g(x), \; x \neq 0, \\[2mm] k \text{ an arbitrary constant.} \end{cases}$

If k = α, then a(x) = 1 for all x ≠ 0. But then we must also have a(0) = 1 because if it is not so, then the RHS of (19) will be a discontinuous function of y. Hence, we must have a(x) ≡ 1. Then, (19) gives

$$(23) \qquad g(x+y) = g(x) + g(y), \, x \in \mathbb{R}, \, y \in \mathbb{R}.$$

whose strictly monotonic solutions are only of the form g(x)=c x, x ≠ 0, x ∈ ℝ. If we put this form of g in (10), we get $K_n = H_n$ where H_n is given by (6).

If k ≠ 0, then eliminating g from (19) and (22), we get the functional equation

$$a(x+y) = a(x) \, a(y), \, x \neq 0, \, y \neq 0.$$

Also, a(0) = 1. Since g is strictly monotonic and continuous function, therefore, by (22), a is also a strictly monotonic and continuous function with a(0) = 1. Consequently, we must have

$$a(x) = 2^{\lambda x}, \, \lambda \neq 0, \, x \in R.$$

For the sake of convenience, we choose $\lambda = \alpha - 1$, $\alpha \neq 1$. Then, we get

$$(24) \qquad g(x) = \frac{2^{(\alpha-1)x} - 1}{k}, \, k \neq 0, \, \alpha \neq 1, \, x \in R.$$

This form of g gives (from (10)) $K_n = {}^{\alpha}H_n$ where

$$(25) \quad \begin{bmatrix} H_n (p_1, p_2, ..., p_n) = (1-\alpha)^{-1} \log\left[\sum_{k=1}^{n} p_k^{\alpha} \Big/ \sum_{k=1}^{n} p_k \right], \\ \alpha \neq 1, \end{bmatrix}$$

This form of ${}^{\alpha}H_n$ satisfies (b*) only for $\alpha > 0$. Thus, we arrive at (7). This completes the proof of Theorem 1.

A careful examination of the proof shows that it is enough to assume that g is strictly monotonic and continuous function for all $x \in [0, \infty)$ rather than for all $x \in (-\infty, +\infty)$. Then (d*) and (e*) give the translativity equation,

$$(26) \quad \begin{bmatrix} g^{-1}\left[\dfrac{p \; g(-\log_2 p - \log_2 r) + q \; g(-\log_2 q - \log_2 r)}{p + q} \right] \\ g^{-1}\left[\dfrac{p \; g(-\log_2 p + q \; g(-\log_2 q))}{p + q} \right] - \log_2 r, \\ p > 0, q > 0, p + q \leq 1, 0 < r \leq 1. \end{bmatrix}$$

Our problem is to find all continuous and strictly monotonic solutions of (26). In that follows, we shall discuss the solutions of (26) due to Aczel (1964).

Let us put $x = -\log_2 p$ and $y = -\log_2 q$, $t = -\log_2 r$. Then, it is obvious that we must have $x \in (0, \infty)$, $y \in (0, \infty)$, $t \in (0, \infty)$. Also, (26) becomes

(27)
$$
\begin{aligned}
&g^{-1}\left[\frac{2^{-X} g(x+t) + 2^{-y} g(y+t)}{2^{-X} + 2^{-y}}\right] \\
&= g^{-1}\left[\frac{2^{-X} g(x) + 2^{-y} g(y)}{2^{-X} + 2^{-y}}\right] + t, \\
&(2^{-X} + 2^{-y} \leq 1, t \geq 0)
\end{aligned}
$$

Let us put $h_t(x) = g(x+t)$, $x \geq 0$. Then h_t is also a strictly monotonic and continuous function and

(28) $\qquad h^{-1}(z) = g^{-1}(z) - t.$

Consequently, (27) transforms into

(29)
$$
\begin{aligned}
&h^{-1}\left[\frac{2^{-X} h_t(x) + 2^{-y} h_t(y)}{2^{-X} + 2^{-y}}\right] \\
&= g^{-1}\left[\frac{2^{-X} g(x) + 2^{-y} g(y)}{2^{-X} + 2^{-y}}\right], \\
&2^{-X} + 2^{-y} \leq 1,
\end{aligned}
$$

We prove that (29) holds if and only if

(30)
$$
\begin{aligned}
&h_t(x) = A(t) g(x) + B(t), \\
&A(t) \neq 0, B(t) \text{ arbitrary constants.}
\end{aligned}
$$

Now we prove that the only continuous solutions of (29) are of the form (30). Let us introduce a function

(31)
$$\left[\begin{array}{l} \phi_t(x) = h_t(x) - A(t)\, g(x) - B(t), \\[4pt] x \in [0,\infty). \end{array} \right.$$

Then, ϕ_t satisfies (29). Also,

(32)
$$\left[\begin{array}{l} \phi_t\!\left[g^{-1}\!\left[\dfrac{2^{-x}g(x)\ +\ 2^{-y}g(y)}{2^{-x}\ +\ 2^{-y}} \right] \right] \\[14pt] = \dfrac{2^{-x}\phi_t(x)\ +\ 2^{-y}\phi_t(y)}{2^{-x}\ +\ 2^{-y}}, \\[14pt] 2^{-x} + 2^{-y} \le 1. \end{array} \right.$$

Note that ϕ_t is a continuous but not necessarily strictly monotonic function. Let us choose the function ϕ_t such that $\phi_t(1) = \phi_t(2) = 0$. This gives

(33)
$$\left[\begin{array}{l} h_t(1) = A(t)\, g(1) + B(t), \\[4pt] h_t(2) = A(t)\, g(2) + B(t). \end{array} \right.$$

Since g is a strictly monotonic function, therefore, $g(1) - g(2) \neq 0$. Hence, (33) has a unique solution because the determinant of the coefficients is non–zero. Now we prove that $\phi_t(x) \equiv 0$. Let us introduce the notations

$$(34) \quad \begin{cases} x \diamond y = g^{-1} \left[\dfrac{2^{-x} \, g(x) + 2^{-y} \, g(y)}{2^{-x} + 2^{-y}} \right], \\[3em] x \,\square\, y = \dfrac{2^{-x} \, \phi(x) + 2^{-y} \, \phi(y)}{2^{-x} + 2^{-y}}. \end{cases}$$

Then, (32) reduces to

$$(35) \quad \phi_t(x \diamond y) = x \,\square\, y, \quad 2^{-x} + 2^{-y} \leq 1,$$

From now on, as it is clear from (35), we may suppress the suffix t of ϕ_t and write ϕ_t simply as ϕ.

Now, we notice that $x \diamond y$ as a function of two variables is continuous and moreover $x \diamond y \in (x,y)$. Also $x \,\square\, y$ as a function of two variables is continuous but $x \,\square\, y \in (\phi(x), \phi(y))$. Since $x \diamond y = y \diamond x$ and $x \,\square\, y = y \,\square\, x$, therefore, there is no need to distinguish between the ordered pairs (u,v) and (v,u).

Now we proceed further to show that $\phi(x) \equiv 0$ for all $x \in (0,\infty)$.

To begin with, we prove that $\phi(x) = 0$ for all $x \in [1,2]$. If not, suppose there exists an $x \in [1,2]$ such that $\phi(x_1) \neq 0$. Let

$$\begin{cases} E_1 = \{x \colon x \in \{1,x_1) \text{ and } \phi(x) = 0\}, \\[0.5em] E_2 = \{x \colon x \in (x_1,2] \text{ and } \phi(x) = 0\}. \end{cases}$$

Then E_1 has an upper limit c_1 and E_2 has a lower limit c_2 and since ϕ is continuous, therefore, $c_1 \in E_1$ and $c_2 \in E_2$. Then $\phi(x) \neq 0$ for all $x \in (c_1, c_2)$ whereas $\phi(c_1) = \phi(c_2) = 0$. But, by (35),

$$\phi(c_1 \diamond c_2) = c_1 \square c_2.$$

Since $c_1 \square c_2 \in (\phi(c_1), \phi(c_2))$ and $\phi(c_1) = \phi(c_2) = 0$, therefore $c_1 \square c_2 = 0$. On the other hand, $\phi(c_1 \diamond c_2) \neq 0$. Thus, we arrive at a contradiction. Thus $\phi(x) = 0$ for all $x \in [1,2]$.

Now we prove that $\phi(x) = 0$ for all $x > 2$. Let

$$D = \{x: x \geq 2 \text{ and } \phi(x) = 0\}.$$

If this set had an upper limit say c_3, then it will belong to D and then by applying the above sort of arguments, one can conclude that for all $x \in [2, c_3]$ we have $\phi(x) = 0$ and consequently $\phi(x) = 0$ for all $x \in [1, c_3]$. But $\phi(x) \neq 0$ for all $x > c_3$. Because of the continuity of the operation '$\diamond$', there must exist come $x_1 > c_3$ but sufficiently near to c_3 such that $1 \diamond x \in (1, c_3]$ because if for all $x > c_3$, we have $1 \diamond x > c_3$; then by the continuity of the operation, $1 \diamond c_3 \geq c_3$ must hold which is a contradiction to the fact that $1 \diamond c_3 \in (1, c_3)$. Now,

$$\phi(1 \diamond x_1) = 0, \ \phi(1) \neq 0, \ \phi(x_1) \neq 0.$$

Then,

$$0 = \phi(1 \diamond x_1) = 1 \square x_1 \notin (0, \phi(x_1))$$

which is again a contradiction. Thus we conclude that $\phi(x) = 0$ for all $x \in [1,\infty)$ and hence for all $x > 2$.

Finally, we prove that $\phi(x) = 0$ for all $x \in [0,1)$. Let c_4 be the smallest value of x for which $\phi(x) = 0$ for all $x > c_4$. Then $\phi(c_4) = 0$. We claim that $c_4 = 0$. If possible, let $c_4 > 0$. Then we will have $\phi(x) = 0$ for all $x \geq c_4$. On the other hand, since $\phi(x) \neq 0$ for all $x < c_4$, therefore, we can always find a sequence $< d_n >_{n=1}^{\infty}$ such that $d_n \uparrow c_4$ and $\phi(d_n) \neq 0$. Choose a number $r > - \log (1-2^{-c_4})$. Then $c_4 > - \log(1-2^{-r}) = c_5$ and for some $x_0 \in (c_5, c_4)$ but sufficiently close to c_4, $x_0 \diamond r \geq x_4$. But, by supposition, $\phi(x_0 \diamond r) = 0$, $\phi(r) = 0$ whereas $\phi(x_0) \neq 0$ which is a contradiction to (35). Hence $c_4 = 0$ and thus $\phi(x) = 0$ for all $x > 0$.

Thus, it has been proved that $\phi(x) = 0$ for all $x \in [0,\infty)$. Then, (31) gives

$$h_t(x) = A(t)\, g(x) + B(t)$$

or equivalently

$$g(x+t) = A(t)\, g(x) + B(t).$$

1.2.2 The Aczel – Daroczy Characterization

In this section, we shall discuss a functional equation which enables us to characterize simultaneously the Shannon entropy and the Rényi entropy. We shall restrict only to complete probability distributions i.e.,

$$(p_1, p_2, ..., p_n), \; p_i > 0, \sum_{i=1}^{n} p_i = 1$$

and our discussion will be restricted to all positive integer $n = 2, 3, ...$ Note that $n = 1$ is a trivial case.

Since $p_i > 0$, $i = 1, 2, ..., n$, $\sum_{i=1}^{n} p_i = 1$, therefore, the Shannon entropy may be written in the form

(1) $$H_n(p_1, p_2, ..., p_n) = - \log \left[\prod_{i=1}^{n} p_i^{\; p_i} \right]$$

Likewise, the Rényi entropy may be written in the form

(2) $$H_n(p_1, p_2, ..., p_n) = - \log \left[\sum_{i=1}^{n} p_i^{\alpha} \right]^{\alpha - 1}, \; \alpha \neq 1.$$

Note that since each p_i is positive, therefore, there is no need to restrict to $\alpha > 0$. The additivity property of both the Shannon and the Rényi entropies give

(3)
$$\prod_{j-1}^{m} \prod_{i=1}^{n} (p_i q_j)^{p_i q_j} = \left[\prod_{i=1}^{n} p_i^{p_i} \right] \left[\prod_{j=1}^{m} q_j^{q_j} \right]$$

and

(4)
$$\left[\sum_{i=1}^{n} \sum_{j=1}^{m} (p_i q_j)^{\alpha} \right]^{\frac{1}{\alpha-1}} = \left[\sum_{i=1}^{n} p_i^{\alpha} \right]^{\frac{1}{\alpha-1}}$$
$$\left[\sum_{j=1}^{m} q_j \right]^{\frac{1}{\alpha-1}},$$

(5)
$$\begin{cases} f^{-1} \left[\sum_{i=1}^{n} \sum_{j=1}^{m} p_i q_j \, f(p_i q_j) \right] \\ \\ = f^{-1} \left[\sum_{i=1}^{n} p_i \, f(p_i) \right] f^{-1} \left[\sum_{j=1}^{m} q_j \, f(q_j) \right], \\ \\ p_i > 0, \, q_j > 0, \, i = 1,2,...,n; \, j = 1,2,...,m; \\ \\ m,n = 2,3,..; \, \sum_{i=1}^{n} p_i = \sum_{j=1}^{m} q_j = 1 \end{cases}$$

where f: $(0,1) \to \mathbb{R}$ is a strictly monotonic and continuous function and f^{-1} denotes the inverse function of f.

Below, we find all possible continuous solutions of (5) and the treatment presented here is due to Aczel and Daroczy (1963).

Let us put $q_j = \frac{1}{m}$, $j = 1,2,...,m$. Then (5) reduces to

$$(6) \qquad m\, f^{-1}\left[\sum_{i=1}^{n} p_i\, f(\frac{p_i}{m})\right] = f^{-1}\left[\sum_{i=1}^{n} p_i\, f(p_i)\right].$$

If we set $f_m(x) = f(\frac{x}{m})$ which means $f_m^{-1}(z) = m\, f^{-1}(z)$, then (6) reduces to

$$(7) \qquad \begin{cases} f^{-1}\left[\sum_{i=1}^{n} p_i\, f(p_i)\right] = f_m^{-1}\left[\sum_{i=1}^{n} p_i\, f_m(p_i)\right], \\[2mm] p_i > 0, i = 1,2,...,n,\ \sum_{i=1}^{n} p_i = 1,\ n = 2,3,... \end{cases}$$

If we write $f_m = h$ for the sake of convenience, then (7) reduces to

$$(8) \qquad \begin{cases} f^{-1}\left[\sum_{i=1}^{n} p_i\, f(p_i)\right] = \left[\sum_{i=1}^{n} p_i\, G(f(p_i))\right] \\[2mm] p_i > 0,\ i = 1,2,...,n;\ \sum_{i=1}^{n} p_i = 1,\ n = 2,3,... \end{cases}$$

We prove that (8)

$$(9) \qquad h(x) = A\, f(x) + B,\ A \neq 0,\ B \text{ arbitrary constant.}$$

It is easy to see that (9) satisfies (8). Now we prove that the continuous solutions of (8) are of the form (9).

Let us put

(10) $G(x) = h[f^{-1}(x)], \ x \ \epsilon \ (0,1]$

Then, (8) reduces to

(11) $G \left[\sum_{i=1}^{n} p_i \, f(p_i) = \sum_{i=1}^{n} p_i \, G(f(p_i)) \right]$

Since f is continuous, therefore, so is h and hence so is G. We show that (11) can hold if and only if

(12) $\begin{cases} G(x) = Ax + B, \\ A \neq 0, \text{ B arbitrary constant.} \end{cases}$

It is clear that (12) does satisfy (11). To prove that G can only be of the form (11), we proceed as follows:

    Step 1. First of all, we observe that if G is a solution of (11), then

(13) $\begin{cases} G^*(x) = G(x) - (Ax+B), \\ A \neq 0, \text{ B arbitrary constant, } x \ \epsilon \ (0,1)] \end{cases}$

is also a solution of (11). Now

$$G^* \left[\sum_{i=1}^{n} p_i \, f(p_i) \right]$$

$$= G \left[\sum_{i=1}^{n} p_i\, f(p_i) \right] - \left[A \sum_{i=1}^{n} p_i\, f(p_i) + B \right]$$

$$= \sum_{i=1}^{n} p_i\, G(f(p_i)) - \sum_{i=1}^{n} p_i\, [A\, f(p_i) + B]$$

$$= \sum_{i=1}^{n} p_i\, [G(f(p_i)) - (Af(p_i) + B)]$$

$$= \sum_{i=1}^{n} p_i\, G^*(f(p_i))$$

Thus G^* also satisfies (11). Also, G^* is a continuous function because G is a continuous function.

Step 2. For certain u and v (to be specified later on), G^* satisfies Jensen's equality, that is,

$$(14) \qquad G^*\!\left(\frac{u+v}{2}\right) = \frac{G^*(u)+G^*(v)}{2}.$$

Let us choose $n = m+1$, $p_i = x_i$, $i = 1,2,...,m$ and $p_{m+1} = \frac{1}{2}$, $\sum_{i=1}^{m} x_i = \frac{1}{2}$. Then, we have

$$(15) \qquad \begin{bmatrix} G^*\!\left[\sum_{i=1}^{m} x_i\, f(x_i) + \tfrac{1}{2} f(\tfrac{1}{2}) \right] \\[2mm] = \sum_{i=1}^{m} x_i\, G^*(f(x_i)) + \tfrac{1}{2}\, G^*(f(\tfrac{1}{2})). \end{bmatrix}$$

Now, choose $n = 2m$, $p_i = x_i$, $i = 1, 2, ..., n$; and

$$p_{n+1} = y_i, i = 1, 2, ..., n; \sum_{i=1}^{m} x_i = \sum_{i=1}^{m} y_i = \tfrac{1}{2}.$$

Then,

(16)
$$\left[G^* \left[\sum_{i=1}^{m} x_i \, f(x_i) + \sum_{i=1}^{m} y_i \, f(y_i) \right] \right.$$

$$\left. = \sum_{i=1}^{m} x_i \, G^*(f(x_i)) + \sum_{i=1}^{m} y_i \, G^*(f(y_i)).$$

Let us choose

(17)
$$u = 2 \sum_{i=1}^{m} x_i \, f(x_i), \quad v = 2 \sum_{i=1}^{m} y_i \, f(y_i)$$

and write

$$\tfrac{1}{2} f(\tfrac{1}{2}) = c.$$

Then

$$G^*(\tfrac{u+v}{2}) \quad = G^* \left[\sum_{i=1}^{m} x_i \, f(x_i) + \sum_{i=1}^{m} y_i \, f(y_i) \right]$$

$$= \sum_{i=1}^{m} x_i \, G^*(f(x_i)) + \sum_{i=1}^{m} y_i \, G^*(f(y_i))$$

$$\left[= G^* \left[\sum_{i=1}^{m} x_i \, f(x_i) + c \right] - \tfrac{1}{2} G^*(2c) \right.$$

$$\left. + G^* \left[\sum_{i=1}^{m} y_i \, f(y_i) + c \right] - \tfrac{1}{2} G^*(2c) \right.$$

$$= G^*(\frac{u}{2} + c) + G^*(\tfrac{1}{2}v + c) - G^*(2c).$$

If we now put u = v, we get

$$G^*(u) = 2G^*(\frac{u}{2} + c) - G^*(2c)$$

Hence,

$$G^*(\frac{u+v}{2}) \quad \begin{bmatrix} = \tfrac{1}{2}G^*(u) + \tfrac{1}{2}G^*(2c) + \tfrac{1}{2}G^*(v) \\ \\ + \tfrac{1}{2}G^*(2c) - G^*(2c) \end{bmatrix}$$

$$= \frac{G^*(u) + G^*(v)}{2}$$

Thus, G* satisfies (14).

So far we have shown that (14) holds only for values u and v which are of the form (17). Now we show that, in fact, (17) holds for all u ∈ (f[1/2n], f[1/2]), v ∈ (f[1/2n], f[1/2]).

Step 3. $G^*(u) = 0$ for all u ∈ $(0, \tfrac{1}{2}]$.

Let us consider the function F defined as

(18)

$$\begin{bmatrix} F(x_1, x_2, ..., x_n) = 2 \sum_{i=1}^{n} f^*(x_i), \\ \\ x_i \geq 0,\ i = 1, 2, ..., m,\ \sum_{i=1}^{m} x_i = \tfrac{1}{2} \end{bmatrix}$$

where

(19) $f^*(x)$ $\begin{cases} = f(x), \ x \in (0,1] \\ = 0, \ \ x = 0. \end{cases}$

Then, F is a continuous function of its arguments and achieves every value between

$$F(\frac{1}{2m},\frac{1}{2m},...,\frac{1}{2m}) = f(\frac{1}{2m}), \ F(\tfrac{1}{2},0,0,...,0) = f(\tfrac{1}{2}).$$

Thus, the Jensen equality (141 will hold for all $u \in [f[\frac{1}{2m}], f[\frac{1}{2}])$, $v \in [f[\frac{1}{2m}], f[\frac{1}{2}])$. Since G^* is continuous, and since every continuous solution of (14) is linear, therefore,

(20) $\begin{cases} G^*(u) = A_1 u + B_2, \ u \in [f(1/2m), f(1/2)), \\ m = 2,3,...; \ A_1 \text{ and } B_1 \text{ are arbitrary constants.} \end{cases}$

Now, for any $x \in (0,\tfrac{1}{2})$, there exists a positive integer m such that $x > 1/2m$. Hence,

(21) $G^*(u) = A_1 u + B_1$ for all $u \in (0,\tfrac{1}{2})$.

Using the fact that h is continuous at $u = f(\tfrac{1}{2})$, we conclude that

(22) $G^*(u) = A_1 u + B_1$ for all $u \in (0,\tfrac{1}{2}]$.

From (13) and (22), it follows that

(23) $A_1 x + B_1 = G(x) - (Ax + B).$

Let us choose the constants A $\neq$ 0 and B such that

$$G^*(f(\tfrac{1}{2})) = G^*(f(\tfrac{1}{4})) = 0.$$

Such a choice is possible because the equations

$$Af(\tfrac{1}{2}) + B = G(f(\tfrac{1}{2}))$$

$$Af(\tfrac{1}{4}) + B = G(f(\tfrac{1}{4}))$$

has a non—vanishing determinant. Then, we have $A_1f(\tfrac{1}{2}) + B_1$
$= 0$ and $A_1f(\tfrac{1}{4}) + B_1 = 0$. Because of the strict monotony of f,
it follows that $A_1 = 0$ and then $B_1 = 0$ so that

(24) $G^*(u) = 0$ for all $u \in (0,\tfrac{1}{2}]$.

Step 4 $G^*(u) = 0$ for all $u \in (\tfrac{1}{2},1)$.

Let us choose x) $\in (\tfrac{1}{2},1)$ arbitrarily. Take n = 3 and choose
$p_1 = x_0$, $p_2 = p_3 = \left[\dfrac{1-x_0}{2}\right] < \tfrac{1}{2}$. Then, since G^* satisfies (11),
we have

(25)

$$\begin{aligned}
&G^*[x_0f(x_0) + (1-x_0)\, f\left[\tfrac{1-x_0}{2}\right]] \\
&= x_0G^*(f(x_0)) + (1-x_0)G^*(f\left[\tfrac{1-x_0}{2}\right]) \\
&= x_0G^*(f(x_0)).
\end{aligned}$$

Since f is continuous and strictly monotonic, therefore, there exists an x_1 such that

$$\begin{cases} f(x_1) = x_0 f(x_0) + (1-x_0)\, f\left[\frac{1-x_0}{2}\right], \\ x_1 \in (\frac{1-x_0}{2}, x_0) \end{cases}$$

so that (25) becomes

$$(26) \qquad G^*(f(x_1)) = x_0\, G^*(f(x_0))$$

If $x_1 \leq 1/2$, then, by step 3, $G^*(f(x_1)) = 0$ and hence $G^*(f(x_0)) = 0$. If $x_1 > 1/2$, then, by the above procedure, we can again obtain the equation

$$G^*(x_1 f(x_1) + (1-x_1)f(\frac{1-x_1}{2})) = x_1\, G^*(f(x_1))$$

and then put

$$f(x_2) = x_1 f(x_1) + (1-x_1)f(\frac{1-x_1}{2}), \quad \frac{1-x_1}{2} < x_2 < x_1 < x_0.$$

If $x_2 \leq 1/2$, then by the use of step 3, $G^*(f(x_2)) = 0$ and consequently $G^*(f(x_1)) = 0$ and hence $G^*(f(x_0)) = 0$. If $x_2 > 1/2$, then we can introduce a third point x_3 and then continue the above arguments indefinitely. In this way, we get a sequence $< x_j >_{j=0}^{\infty}$ defined recursively by

$$(27) \qquad \begin{cases} f(x_n) = x_{n-1}\, f(x_{n-1}) + (1-x_{n-1})\, f(\frac{1-x_{n-1}}{2}), \\ n = 1,2,\dots \end{cases}$$

We prove that there always exists a positive integer n_0 such that $x_{n_0} \leq 1/2$ and

(28) $\qquad G^*(f(x_k)) = x_{k-1} G^*(f(x_{k-1})), \ k = 1,2,...,n_0$

from which it follows that $G^*(f(x_0)) = 0$.

If possible, suppose there does not exist any such n_0 for which $n_{x_0} \leq 1/2$. This means that $x_n < 1/2$ for all n. Then $\frac{1-x_n}{2} < 1/2 < x_n$ for all n and consequently, by (27), we have

$$f(x_{n+1}) = x_n f(x_n) + (1-x_n) f(\frac{1-x_n}{2})$$
or $\qquad f(x_n) \quad = x_n f(x_n) + (1-x_n) f(x_n)$

according as f is strictly monotonic decreasing or increasing. This means that in both cases we have $x_{n+1} < x_n$. Thus $<x_j>_j^\infty = 0$ is a decreasing sequence. It is obviously bounded below by 1/2. Hence it converges and has a limit, say x^*. Then $1 > x^* = \lim_{n \to \infty} x_n \geq \frac{1}{2}$. Now, we let $n \to \infty$ in (27). Then, we get (using the continuity of f)

$$f(x^*) = x^* f(x^*) + (1-x^*) f(\frac{1-x^*}{2})$$

from which it follows that $f(x^*) = f(\frac{1-x^*}{2})$. Since f is strictly monotonic, therefore, $x^* = \frac{1-x^*}{2} \Rightarrow x^* = 1/3 < 1/2$, which is a contradiction to the fact that $x^* = \lim_{n \to \infty} x_n \geq \frac{1}{2}$. Hence we conclude that there always exists a positive integer n_0 with the above mentioned desired properties. Thus $G^*(f(x)) = 0$ for all $x \in (\frac{1}{2}, 1)$. The fact that $G^*(f(x)) = 0$ follows by continuity of G^*. Thus, we have

Step 5 $\qquad$ $G^*(u) = 0$, for all $u \in (0,1]$.

With this discussion, it now follows from (13) that G is only of the form (12). Now, it follows from our notations and the equations (7), (10) and (11) that

(29)
$$
\begin{cases}
f(\frac{x}{m}) = A(m)\, f(x) + B(m), \ x \in (0,1], \\
m = 2,3,..., A(m) \neq 0.
\end{cases}
$$

[The functional equation (29) may be extended to $m = 1$ by putting $A(1) = 1$ and $B(1) = 0$.] Our object is to find all continuous solutions of (29), of course, f: $(0,1] \to \mathbb{R}$ is strictly monotonic also. Let us write $x = \frac{1}{t}$, $t \in [1,\infty)$. Then (29) reduces to

(30)
$$
\begin{cases}
f(\frac{1}{tm}) = A(m)\, f(\frac{1}{t}) + B(m), \ t \in [1,\infty), \\
m = 1,2,3,..., A(m) \neq 0.
\end{cases}
$$

If we put

(31) $\qquad$ $f_1(t) = f(\frac{1}{t})$, $t \in [1,\infty)$,

then (30) reduces to

(32)
$$\begin{cases} f_1(tm) = A(m) \, f_1(t) + B(m), \\ t \in [1, \infty), \ m = 1,2,3,\dots \end{cases}$$

Let us put $t = 1$. Then, we get

(33) $\qquad f_1(m) = A(m) \, f_1(1) + B(m), \ m = 1,2,3,\dots$

From (32) and (33), we get

$$f_1(tm) - f_1(m) = A(m) \, [f_1(t) - f(1)]$$

Thus, if we put
(34) $\qquad f_2(t) = f_1(t) - f_1(1),$

we get
(35)
$$\begin{cases} f_2(tm) = A(m) f_2(t) + f_2(m), \\ t \in [1, \infty), \ m = 1,2,\dots \end{cases}$$

Also, from (34), we get $f_2(1) = 0$. Now, let us put $t = n$, where n is a positive integer. Then (35) gives

(36) $\qquad [A(m)-1] \, f_2(n) = [A(n)-1] \, f_2(m); \ m,n = 1,2,\dots$

Let us fix $n = 2$. Since f is strictly monotonic and continuous, therefore, f_1 and f_2 are both continuous and strictly monotonic.

Since $f_2(1) = 0$, therefore $f_2(2) \neq 0$. Consequently, with $\lambda = \frac{A(2)-1}{f_2(2)}$, (37) gives $A(m) = \lambda f_2(m) = 1$. Consequently, (35) reduces to

$$(38) \qquad \begin{cases} f_2(tm) = \lambda f_2(m)f_2(t) + f_2(t)+f_2(m), \\[2mm] m = 1,2,... \text{ and } t \in [1,\infty) \end{cases}$$

We distinguish two cases:

$$\text{Case 1} \qquad \lambda = 0. \text{ Then (38) reduces to}$$

$$(39) \qquad f_2(tm) = f_2(t) + f_2(m); \; t \in [1,\infty), \, m = 1,2,...$$

With $t = n$, $n = 1,2,...$, we get the number–theoretic equation

$$(40) \qquad f_2(nm) = f_2(n) + f_2(m); \, n,m = 1,2,3,...$$

Now,

$$\lim_{m \to \infty} \{f_2(m + 1) - f_2(m)\}$$

$$= \lim_{m \to \infty} \{f_2(1 + \frac{1}{m})] - f_2(m)\}$$

$$= \lim_{m \to \infty} \{f_2(m) + f_2(1 + \frac{1}{m}) - f_2(m)\}$$

$$= \lim_{m \to \infty} \{f_2(1 + \frac{1}{m})\}$$

$$= f_2 \{\lim_{m \to \infty} (1 + \frac{1}{m})\} = f_2(1) = 0.$$

Hence, by Lemma 6 of 1.1.1, $f_2(m) = a \log_2 m$ where $a \neq 0$ is an arbitrary constant. Now, let $t = \frac{k}{m}$ where $k \geq m$ and k is an integer. Then

$$
\begin{aligned}
a \log_2 k &= f_2(k) = f_2(\frac{k}{m} \, m) \\
&= f_2(\frac{k}{m}) + f_2(m) \\
&= f_2(\frac{k}{m}) + a \log_2 m
\end{aligned}
$$

so that

$$f_2(t) = a \log_2 t \text{ for all rational } t \in [1,\infty).$$

Then, by the continuity of f_2, it follows that

(41) $\qquad f_2(t) = a \log_2 t, \ t \in [1,\infty).$

From (31), (34) and (41), we conclude that

$$f(x) = a \log_2 x + b; \ a \neq 0, \ b \text{ arbitrary constant.}$$

Case 2 $\qquad \lambda \neq 0$. Then, setting $h_1(t) = \lambda f_1(t) + 1$, (38) reduces to

(42) $\qquad h_1(tm) = h_1(t) \, h_1(m); \ t \in [1,\infty), \ m = 1,2,\ldots$

If there exists an m, say $m = m_0$, such that $h_1(m_0) = 0$, then (42) gives $h_1(tm_0) = 0$ for all $t \in [1,\infty)$ and consequently $h_1(t) = 0$ for all $t \in [1,\infty)$. But, since f_1 is strictly monotonic, therefore, h_1 is also strictly monotonic. Hence $h_1(t) \equiv 0$ is not possible. Now, let us put $t = m$ in (42). We obtain $h_1(m^2) = [h_1(m)]^2 > 0$. Also, (42) gives

(43) $\qquad h_1(m^2 n^2) = h_1(m^2) \, h_1(n^2).$

Hence, if we put $f_0(m) = \log_2 h_1(m^2)$, we get

(44) $\qquad f_0(mn) = f_0(m) + f_0(n), \quad m,n = 1,2,3,...$

Now,

$$\lim_{m \to \infty} [f_0(m+1) - f_0(m)]$$

$$= \lim_{m \to \infty} \log_2 \left[\frac{h_1[m^2(1 + 1/m)^2]}{h_1(m^2)} \right]$$

$$= \log_2 \lim_{m \to \infty} h_1(1 + 1/m)^2)$$

$$= \log_2 h_1(1) = \log_2 1 = 0.$$

Hence

(45) $\qquad f_0(m) = a \log_2 m, \ a \neq 0$ arbitrary constant.

Then

$$h_1(m^2) = 2^{(a/2) \log_2 m^2}$$

$$= (m^2)^{(a/2)}$$

$$= (m^2)^{1-\alpha}$$

where $\frac{a}{2} = 1-\alpha$, $\alpha \neq 1$. Setting $m = j^2$, $t = \frac{k^2}{j^2}$, $k^2 \geq j^2$, we have

$$(k^2)^{1-\alpha} = h_1(k^2)$$
$$= h_1(\frac{k^2}{j^2} j^2)$$
$$= h_1(\frac{k^2}{j^2}) h_1(j^2)$$
$$= h_1(\frac{k^2}{j^2}) (j^2)^{1-\alpha}$$

so that

$$h_1(t) = t^{1-\alpha} \text{ for all } t = \frac{k^2}{j^2} \in [1,\infty),$$

and then by the continuity of h_1, we get

(46) $\qquad h_1(t) = t^{1-\alpha}, t \in [1,\infty).$

and consequently

$$f_1(t) = \frac{t^{1-\alpha}-1}{\lambda} - f_1(1) \quad \lambda \neq 0$$

or equivalently

$$f(x) = ax^{\alpha-1} + b, \quad a \neq 0, b \text{ arbitrary constant.}$$

Summarizing all these results, we obtain the following theorem:

Theorem 2: *If f: $(0,1] \to \mathbb{R}$ is a strictly monotonic and continuous function which satisfies (5), then f is only of the following two forms*

(47) $f(x) = a \log_2 x + b$

(48) $f(x) = a\, x^{\alpha-1} + b,\ \alpha \neq 1$

where $a \neq 0$ *and* b *are arbitrary constants. In the first case,*

(49) $$f^{-1}\left[\sum_{i=1}^{m} p_i\, f(p_i)\right] = 2^{\sum\limits_{i=1}^{n} p_x \log p_i}$$

and in the second case

(50) $$f^{-1}\left[\sum_{i=1}^{m} p_i\, f(p_i)\right] = \left[\sum_{i=1}^{m} p_i\right]^{\frac{1}{\alpha-1}}$$

The negative of the logarithms of (49) and (50) give the Shannon entropy and the Rényi entropy respectively.

In order to exclude the Rényi entropy of order $\alpha < 0$, all that is needed is to make an additional assumption of the fact that $\lim\limits_{x \to 0^+} xf(x) = 0$. Then

$$\lim_{x \to 0^+} (ax^{\alpha} + bx) = 0$$

is possible only for $\alpha > 0$.

1.2.3 Conditional Rényi Entropy

The restricted applicability of the Rényi entropy $^{\alpha}H_n$, $\alpha > 0$, $\alpha \neq 1$ is made apparent by some inconsistencies which it provides with regard to some measures of conditional entropy. In this section, we discuss these aspects.

Following the pattern of the expression of the Rényi entropy $^{\alpha}H_n$, $\alpha > 0$, $\alpha \neq 1$, it is natural to define the joint entropy

$$
\begin{aligned}
&^{\alpha}H_{nm}(r_{11},r_{21},..,r_{n1};...;r_{1m},r_{2m},...,r_{nm}) \\
&= (1-\alpha)^{-1} \log_2 \left[\sum_{i=1}^{m} \sum_{j=1}^{n} f_{ij} \right], \ \alpha > 0, \ \alpha \neq 1, \\
&(r_{11},r_{21},...,r_{n1};...;r_{1m},r_{21},...,r_{nm}) \in \Delta_{nm}
\end{aligned}
\tag{1}
$$

Thus

$$
^{\alpha}H_{nm}(r_{11},r_{21},..,r_{n1};..;r_{1n},r_{2m},..,r_{nm}) - {^{\alpha}H_n}(p_1,p_2,..,p_n)
$$

$$
= (1-\alpha)^{-1} \log_2 \left[\sum_{i=1}^{n} \left\{ \frac{(p_i)^{\alpha}}{\sum_{i=1}^{n}(p_i)^{\alpha}} \right\} \sum_{j=1}^{m}(r_j/i)^{\alpha} \right]; \ \alpha > 0, \ \alpha \neq 1.
$$

Thus, defining conditional entropy by

(2)

$$
\begin{aligned}
&H_{n,m}[(q_1,q_2,..,q_m)/(p_1,p_2,..,p_n)] \\
&= (1-\alpha)^{-1} \log_2 \left[\sum_{i=1}^{n} \left[\frac{(p_i)^{\alpha}}{\sum_{i=1}^{n}(p_j)^{\alpha}} \right] \sum_{j=1}^{m}(r_{j/i})^{\alpha} \right], \\
&\alpha > 0, \ \alpha \neq 1,
\end{aligned}
$$

we have

(3)

$$
\begin{aligned}
&{}^{\alpha}H_{nm}(r_{11},r_{21},...,r_{n1}; \ ...; \ r_{1m},r_{2m},...,y_{nm}) \\
&= {}^{\alpha}H_n(p_1,p_2,...,p_n) \\
&+ H_{n,m}(q_1,q_2,...,q_m/p_1,p_2,\sim.,p_n), \\
&\alpha > 0, \ \alpha \neq 1.
\end{aligned}
$$

This shows that if conditional entropy

$$
{}^{\alpha}H_{n,m}(q_1,q_2,...,q_m/p_1,p_2,...,p_n)
$$

is defined by (2), then the Rényi entropy is also strongly additive in addition to being additive. In addition to (2), Rényi (1960), also defined another conditional entropy

(4)

$$
\begin{aligned}
&H_{n,m}(q_1,q_2,...,q_m/p_1,p_2,...,p_n) \\
&= (1-\alpha)^{-1} \log_2 \sum_{i=1}^{n} \sum_{j=1}^{m} p_i(r_{j/i})^{\alpha}, \\
&\alpha > 0, \ \alpha \neq 1.
\end{aligned}
$$

The main difference between (2) and (4) is that whereas the former satisfies (3), the latter does not satisfy

$$
(5) \quad
\begin{bmatrix}
{}^{\alpha}H_{n,m}\big(r_{11}, r_{21}, .., r_{n1}; \ ...; \ r_{1m}, r_{2m}, ..., r_{nm}\big) \\
\\
= {}^{\alpha}H_{n}(p_1, p_2, .., p_m) + H_{n,m}(q_1, q_2, .., q_m / p_1, p_2, .., p_n) \\
\\
\alpha > 0, \ \alpha \neq 1.
\end{bmatrix}
$$

Indeed, assume momentarily that (5) is satisfied. Then, for $n = m = 2$, after certain manipulations, it follows that

$$
p_1^{\alpha-1} = (1-p_1)^{\alpha-1}
$$

which is impossible since $\alpha \neq 1$.

Another main difference between (2) and (4) is that ${}^{\alpha}H_{n,m}$ satisfies the inequality

$$
\begin{bmatrix}
{}^{\alpha}H_{n,m}(q_1, q_2, .., q_m / p_1, p_2, .., p_n) \leq {}^{\alpha}H_m(q_1, q_2, .., q_m), \\
\\
\alpha > 0, \ \alpha \neq 1.
\end{bmatrix}
$$

where ${}^{\alpha}H_{n,m}$, defined by (2) does not satisfy this inequality. On the other hand, it is interesting to note that

(6)

$$
\begin{cases}
\lim_{\alpha \to 1} {}^{\alpha}H_{n,m}(q_1,q_2,..,q_m/p_1,p_2,..,p_n) \\[2ex]
= \lim_{\alpha \to 1} {}^{\alpha}H_{n,m}(q_1,q_2,..,q_m) \\[2ex]
= \sum_{i=1}^{n} \sum_{j=1}^{m} r_{ij} \log_2 r_{j/i} \\[2ex]
= H_{n,m}(q_1,q_2,..,q_m/p_1,p_2,..,p_n)
\end{cases}
$$

1.2.4 Properties of the Rényi Entropy

In this section, we list some algebraic and analytic properties of the Rényi entropy. We shall restrict strictly to $\alpha > 0$, $\alpha \neq 1$.

P_1 ${}^{\alpha}H_n$: $\Delta_n \to \mathbb{R}$, $n = 1,2,...$ is a continuous function of its arguments

P_2 ${}^{\alpha}H_n$: $\Delta_n \to \mathbb{R}$, $n = 2,3,...$ is a symmetric function of its arguments

P_3 For all positive integers n,

$$
\begin{cases}
{}^{\alpha}H_{n+1}(p_1,p_2,..,p_n,0) = {}^{\alpha}H_n(p_1,p_2,..,p_n), \\[2ex]
(p_1,p_2,..,p_n) \in \Delta_n; \; (p_1,p_2,..,p_n,0) \in \Delta_{n+1}.
\end{cases}
$$

P_4 $^{\alpha}H_2(\tfrac{1}{2},\tfrac{1}{2}) = 1.$

P_5 $^{\alpha}H_2(1,0) = {}^{\alpha}H_2(0,1) = 0.$

P_6 $^{\alpha}H_n$ is additive for all positive integers i.e.

$$
\begin{cases}
{}^{\alpha}H_{nm}(p_1q_1,..,p_1q_m;\ p_2q_1,..,p_2q_m;\ ...;p_nq_1,..,p_nq_m) \\[2mm]
= {}^{\alpha}H_n(p_1,p_2,..,p_n) + {}^{\alpha}H_m(p_1,p_2,..,p_m), \\[2mm]
(p_1,p_2,..,p_n) \in \Delta_n \text{ and } (q_1,q_2,...,q_m) \in \Delta_m; \\[2mm]
m,n = 1,2,3,....
\end{cases}
$$

P_7 For all positive inter n,

$$
^{\alpha}H_n(p_1,p_2,...,p_n) \le \log_2 n
$$

with equality if and only, if $p_1 = p_2 = ... = p_n = \tfrac{1}{n}.$

P_8 $^{\alpha}H_n$ is not subadditive. (Compare it with the Shannon entropy which is subadditive)

P_9 $^{\alpha}H_n$ is not recursive i.e., it does not satisfy an equation of the form (4) of 1 1.4.

PART TWO

MEASURES OF NONADDITIVE ENTROPY

2.0 INTRODUCTION

The Shannon and the Rényi entropies are additive and, during the past three or so decades, researchers have tried to obtain numerous generalizations of those entropies keeping in view that their generalizations are also additive.

Our present objective is to study some nonadditive measures of entropy. Research in this area began with Havrda and Charvat (1967) and quite independently by Behara (1968), and later by Behara and Nath (1971). The Havrda–Charvat formulation of nonadditive entropies depends on an axiomatization which rests on the methods of functional equations. The nonadditive measures of entropy, however, can be introduced without the use of functional equations, as proposed and carried out in Behara (1968) and Behara and Nath (1971, 1973). The method is based on the geometry of entropy measures which accounts for the introduction of the term "*geometric entropy*".

While trying to introduce nonadditive measures of entropy by using geometric ideas, we do not need to assume, unlike in the method of functional equations, the properties of recursivity, additivity etc. And, rather importantly, we do not need to assume the prior existence of the parameter in the derivation of entropy measures by our *geometric method*. We also provide a characterization of a nonadditivity entropy using a functional equation without assuming the prior existence of the parameter [Behara and Nath (1974)].

It may be argued, at least from a theoretical point of view, that the nonadditive measure of entropy deserves more attention, due to its general character, than it currently receives. The Shannon entropy happens to be a limiting case of the nonadditive entropies. The Rényi entropy can be easily derived from a nonadditive entropy. The work in the applications of nonadditive entropies in coding theory [Nath (1975)] as well as ergodic theory [Chawla (1974)] has begun recently.

The geometric representations of nonadditive entropies, derivation of which is based on a minimum number of axioms, envelopes not only the class of additive entropies but also promises to deliver all possible measures of entropies, both additive and nonadditive.

We may therefore call all measures of entropy admitting geometric representation as *geometric entropy*.

We shall study nonadditive entropies under the following classes: Algebraic entropy (polynomial and nonpolynomial entropies) and transcendental entropy. The latter entropy, so far the only entropy other than the Shannon entropy has proved its usefulness in the study of isomorphism problem of Bernoulli Shifts, under the celebrated Kolmogorov–Ornstein theorem [Chawla (1974)] in ergodic theory.

Polynomial entropies have also been studied as semivaluations on lattices [Behara and Chawla (1979)].

There is a host of measures associated with or derived from various measures of entropy. An account of measures of *directed divergence*, derived from polynomial entropy is given in Behara and Nath (1980).

2.1 POLYNOMIAL ENTROPY

We shall study the geometry concerning the Shannon and Rényi entropies and then introduce a nonadditive measure of entropy by using simple algebraic and geometric ideas. Let us consider

(1)
$$\begin{cases} \omega(p) = H_2(p, 1-p) \\ = -p \log_2 p - (1-p) \log_2(1-p), \quad 0 \le p \le 1, \end{cases}$$

where $\omega: [0,1] \to \mathbb{R}$. It is easily seen that

(2) $\omega(0) = 0,\ \omega(1) = 0,\ \omega(\tfrac{1}{2}) = 1.$

Thus, if we draw the graph of the function ω, then, on account of (2), it follows that the graph must pass through the three points

(3) $(0,0),\ (1,0)\ \text{and}\ (\tfrac{1}{2},1).$

From (1), it is also obvious that

(4) $\omega(p) = \omega(1-p),\ 0 \leq p \leq 1,$

from which it follows that

(5) $\omega(\tfrac{1}{2} + \ell) = \omega(\tfrac{1}{2} - \ell),\ 0 \leq \ell \leq \tfrac{1}{2}$

so that the graph of ω is symmetric around the line $p = \tfrac{1}{2}$. Differentiating (1) with respect to $p \in (0,1)$, we notice that

$$\frac{d}{dp}\,\omega(p) = \log_2\!\left(\frac{1-p}{p}\right)$$

from which it follows that ω is a strictly monotonically increasing function of $p \in (0,\tfrac{1}{2})$ and strictly monotonically decreasing function of $p \in (\tfrac{1}{2},1)$. At $p = \tfrac{1}{2}$, $\frac{d}{dp}\,\omega(p) = 1$. On the other hand,

(6) $\lim\limits_{p \to 0} \dfrac{d}{dp}\,\omega(p) = +\infty,\ \ \lim\limits_{p \to 1}\dfrac{d}{dp}\,\omega(p) = -\infty$

so that ω is not differentiable at $p = 0,1$. However, ω is continuous at $p = 0,1$.

Now, let us consider the functions

$$^\beta f : [0,1] \to \mathbb{R}, \quad \beta \neq 1,$$

defined as

(7) $\qquad ^\beta f(p) = (1-\beta)^{-1} \log_2[p^\beta + (1-p)^\beta],$

with the convention $0^r = 0$, $r \in \mathbb{R}$.

Here, again, it is easy to see that

(8) $\qquad ^\beta f(0) = 0, \quad ^\beta f(1) = 0, \quad ^\beta f(\tfrac{1}{2}) = 1,$

so that the graphs of f also pass through the three points $(0,0)$, $(1,0)$ and $(\tfrac{1}{2},1)$ as mentioned in (3). Also,

(9) $\qquad ^\beta f(p) = {}^\beta f(1-p), \quad 0 \leq p \leq 1,$

so that, $^\beta f$ is also symmetric around $p = \tfrac{1}{2}$

Note that,

$$\lim_{\beta \to 1} {}^\beta f = \omega, \quad ^\beta f(\tfrac{1}{2}) = 1.$$

Thus, for $p = \frac{1}{2}$, f is independent of β. In other words, $\beta \rightarrow {}^\beta f(\frac{1}{2})$ is a constant function of $\beta \neq 1$ From these observations, it follows that the graphs of ω and f meet only at the three points mentioned in (3) and, for $p \in (0,1)$, the graph of f lies below or above the graph of ω according as $1 < \beta < \infty$ or $0 < \beta < 1$.

Actual computation gives

$$(10) \qquad \begin{cases} {}^2f(p) = -\log_2 y_2(p) \\ {}^3f(p) = -\log_2 y_3(p), \end{cases}$$

where,

$$(11) \qquad \begin{cases} y_2(p) = 2p^2 - 2p + 1, \\ y_3(p) = 3p^3 - 3p + 1. \end{cases}$$

Both the functions $y_2 \colon [0,1] \rightarrow \mathbb{R}$ and $y_3 \colon [0,1] \rightarrow \mathbb{R}$ represent parabolas geometrically. These parabolas pass through the points $(0,0)$, $(\frac{1}{2},\frac{1}{2})$ and $(1,0)$. From (10), it is obvious that the Rényi entropies ${}^2f = {}^2H_2$ and ${}^3f = {}^3H_2$ are functions of parabolas.

In entropy theory, the mathematical forms of measures of entropy depends upon the set of postulates assumed, taking into consideration the fact that the assumed postulates are independent of each other and are based upon intuition. Both Shannon and Rényi entropies are additive. Below, we are going to investigate some nonadditive measures of entropy for complete probability distributions with only two elements, say

$$p \text{ and } 1-p, \qquad 0 \leq p \leq 1.$$

Let $K_2: \Delta_2 \to \mathbb{R}$ be such that $K_2(p,1-p)$ denotes the entropy of the probability distribution. We assume that K_2 possesses the following properties:

(a_1) $K_2(0,1) = 0$
(a_2) $K_2(\tfrac{1}{2},\tfrac{1}{2}) = 1$
(a_3) $K_2(p,1-p) = K_2(1-p,p), \quad 0 \leq p \leq 1.$

The intuitive explanations of (a_1), (a_2) and (a_3) are provided in 0.3. Let

$$\mathfrak{C} = \{K_2: \Delta_2 \to \mathbb{R}; \ K_2 \text{ satisfies } (a_1), (a_2) \text{ and } (a_3)\}$$

What can be said about the structure of the class $\mathfrak{C}$? Full answer to this question is not known so far. However, it is obvious that $\omega \epsilon \mathfrak{C}$, and $f \epsilon \mathfrak{C}$ for $\beta \neq 1$. But, in addition to these, there are several other functions which also belong to $\mathfrak{C}$.

In mathematical analysis, we know that all real–valued functions are either algebraic or transcendental. The class $\mathfrak{C}$ has both types of functions. Let us first try to investigate algebraic functions.

Let us write $K_2(p,1-p) = {}^\beta h_2(p)$ whenever K_2 is a polynomial of degree β, where β is a positive integer. By (a_1) and (a_2), we also get

(12) $\qquad K_2(0,1) = 0.$

Since the points given in (3) are not collinear, β cannot take the value 1. To overcome this difficulty, we agree to define

(13) $\qquad {}^1h_2(p) = \lim_{\beta \to 1} {}^\beta h_2(p), \quad p \in [0,1].$

Let us take $\beta = 2$. In this case, the most general form of ${}^2h_2$ can be

(14) $\qquad {}^2h_2(p) = c_1 p^2 + c_2 p + c.$

Making use of (3) in the sense that the graph of ${}^2h_2$ should pass through the points listed in (3), it follows that

$$c_1 = -4, \quad c_2 = 4, \quad \text{and } c_3 = 0,$$

so that,

(15) $\qquad \left[\begin{array}{l} {}^2h_2(p) = 4(p - p^2) = \dfrac{p^2 + (1-P)^2 - 1}{c}, \\[2mm] \text{where } c = 2^{1-2} - 1. \end{array} \right.$

In general, we should expect the two–dimensional polynomial entropies to be of the form

(16)
$$\begin{bmatrix} \beta h_2(p) = \dfrac{p^\beta + (1-p)^\beta - 1}{c}, \\ c = 2^{1-\beta} - 1, \quad \beta = 2,3,4,\ldots \end{bmatrix}$$

The polynomials for $\beta = 2,3,4,\ldots$

(17) $$\beta h_2(p) = c_1 p^\beta + c_2 p^{\beta-1} + c\, p^{\beta-2} + \ldots + c_\beta p + c_{\beta+1}$$

give rise to (16) above. Therefore, we call the measure of entropy given in (16) as polynomial entropy.

In what follows we shall give a recent result on polynomial entropy due to Behara (1985).

Let Δ_2 be the set of two–dimensional complete probability distribution given by

(18) $$\Delta_2 = \{(p, 1-p): 0 \le p \le 1\}.$$

Let a real–valued differentiable function f on Δ_2 denote the entropy of the probability distribution and possess the following properties of an information measure:

(a$_1$) $\qquad$ $f(1,0) = f(0,1) = 0$

(a$_2$) $\qquad$ $f(\tfrac{1}{2}.\tfrac{1}{2}) = 1$

(a$_3$) $\qquad$ $f(p, 1-p) = f(1-p, p), \ p\epsilon[0,1].$

We shall study the structure of the class of functions

given by

(19) $\begin{bmatrix} \mathfrak{C}_2 = \{(f)| & f: & \Delta_2 \rightarrow & \mathbb{R}, & \text{differentiable and} \\ \text{satisfying } (a_1), (a_2) \text{ and } (a_3) \}. \end{bmatrix}$

The Shannon entropy

(20) $\mathfrak{S}(\Delta_2) = -\log_2 p - (1-p)\log_2 (1-p)$

as well as the Rényi entropy

(21) $\begin{bmatrix} \mathfrak{R}(\Delta_2) = (1-\alpha)^{-1}\log_2\{p^{\alpha}+(1-p)^{\alpha}\}, \\ \alpha > 0, \ \alpha \neq 1 \end{bmatrix}$

belong to the class $\mathfrak{C}_2$. But in addition to these there are several other functions which belong to $\mathfrak{C}_2$. Therefore, we shall investigate all such real—valued functions. In mathematical analysis, all real—valued functions are either algebraic or transcendental. The class $\mathfrak{C}_2$ of entropies has both these types of functions. We shall first study algebraic functions, and, among algebraic functions the polynomial functions will be considered in this work. The derivation of transcendental entropies such as Shannon and Rényi using methods outlined in this work will be attempted in a future study. Trigonometric entropies in the class of Transcendental entropies have already been derived [Behara and Chorneyko, (accepted)]. We hope, a multitude of new and useful entropies can be derived systematically in this way and then classified according to their various functional properties.

We shall now attempt to derive a formula for a generalized entropy directly from polynomial functions fulfilling the properties of information measures. We shall investigate two—dimensional polynomials here.

Definition 1. *A two—dimensional complete probability polynomial of degree β, where β is a positive integer, is a real—valued function $\mathfrak{B}(\Delta_2)$ given by*

$$(22) \qquad \mathfrak{B}(\Delta_2) \equiv \mathfrak{B}(p) = \sum_{k=0}^{\beta} c_k p^k,$$

where $c_k's$ are the coefficients of p^k, $k = 0, 1,...,\beta$.

Let us write $f(p, 1-p) = \mathfrak{B}(p)$, wherever f is a two—dimensional complete probability polynomial of degree β as in Definition 1.

Now subjecting the two—dimensional polynomial to entropy properties $(a_1),(a_2)$ and (a_3), we observe that the polynomial passes through the points $(0,0)$, $(\frac{1}{2},1)$ and $(1,0)$ and, therefore, $\beta = 1$ is inadmissible. This difficulty, however, is easily overcome by taking the limits.

For $\beta > 2$, we have, by using (a_1), (a_2) and (a_3), and from

(22) the following equations:

(23) $\qquad c_0 = 0$

(24) $\qquad \sum_{k=1}^{\beta} c_k = 0$

(25) $\qquad \sum_{k=0}^{\beta-1} 2^k c_{\beta-k} = 2^\beta.$

We shall call the polynomial in (22) a two–dimensional symmetric complete probability polynomial of degree β, if it fulfills (a_3).

Lemma 1. *For a two–dimensional symmetric complete probability polynomial of degree β,*

(26) $\qquad \mathscr{B}(p) = \sum_{k=0}^{\beta} c_k\, p^k, \; \beta = 2,3,\dots$

we have

(27) $\qquad c_j = (-1)^\beta\, c_{\beta-j} \begin{cases} j = 1,2,\dots,(\beta-2)/2; \; \beta \; even \\[2mm] j = 1,2,\dots,(\beta-1)/2; \; \beta \; odd \end{cases}$

where c_k is the coefficient of p^k, $k = 1,2,\dots,\beta$ in (26).

In order to establish the relationships between the successive coefficients of the polynomial, we have the following

Lemma 2. *For a two-dimensional symmetric complete probability polynomial of degree β,*

$$(28) \qquad \mathcal{B}(p) = \sum_{k=0}^{\beta} c_k \, p^k, \; \beta = 3,4,\ldots$$

we have

$$(29) \qquad \left[\begin{array}{l} c_{j+1} = (-1)^{\beta-j} \, (1/\beta) \, [\binom{\beta}{j+1} c_{\beta-1}], \\[2em] j = 0, 1,\ldots, \beta{-}3. \end{array} \right.$$

where c_k is the coefficient of p^k, $k = 1,2,\ldots,\beta$ in (28).

Proof Upon j^{th} differentiation of (28) with respect to p, we have

$$(30) \qquad \mathcal{B}^{(j)}(p) = \sum_{k=j}^{\beta} \frac{k!}{(k-j)!} \, c_k \, p^{k-j}, \; j = 1,2,\ldots,\beta.$$

Then, by using (27), we have

$$c_{j+1} = (-1)^{\beta-1} \, (1/\beta) \, [\binom{\beta}{j+1} c_{\beta-1}], \; j = 0,2,\ldots,\beta{-}3.$$

Finally, in order to establish the relationship between c_β and $c_{\beta-1}$, we have, by using symmetry, i.e.: (a_3) on (26) and equating the coefficients of p^β and $p^{\beta-1}$, the following

Lemma 3 *For a two−dimensional symmetric complete probability polynomial of degree β, as given in (26), we have*

(31) $\qquad c_{\beta-1} = (\beta/2)\, c_\beta,\ \beta$ *even*

(32) $\qquad c_\beta = 0 \quad,\ \beta$ *odd.*

Now, we are in a position to state the main result for the two−dimensional complete probability polynomial as follows:

Theorem 1 *A two−dimensional complete probability polynomial given by*

$$f(p,\ 1{-}p) \equiv \mathscr{B}(p) = \sum_{k=0}^{\beta} c_k\, p^k,\ \beta = 2,3,..$$

subject to the entropy properties (a_1), (a_2) and (a_3), admits only the form

(34) $\qquad \mathscr{B}(p) = \dfrac{p^\beta + (1-p)^\beta - 1}{2^{1-\beta} - 1},\ \beta = 2,3,...$

which will be called a "two−dimensional polynomial entropy".

Proof Now, using Lemma 2 and Lemma 3 for (26), we have for $\beta = 2,3,...$

$$\mathscr{B}(p) = c_\beta\, p^\beta + c_{\beta-1}\,(1/\beta)\left[\sum_{j+0}^{\beta}(-1)^{\beta-j}\,(^\beta_{j+1})p^{j+1}\right]$$
$$= c_\beta\, p^\beta + (\beta/2)\, c_\beta\,(1/\beta)\,[(1{-}p)^\beta - p^\beta -1]$$

$$= c_\beta \left[p^\beta + (1-p)^\beta - 1 \right]$$

But, by (a_2), we have

$$c_\beta = \frac{1}{2^{1-\beta} - 1}, \, \beta = 2,3,\ldots$$

Therefore,

$$\mathfrak{B}(p) = \frac{p^\beta + (1-p)^\beta - 1}{2^{1-\beta} - 1}, \, \beta = 2,3,\ldots$$

Remark 1   For a positive non–integer β, $(1-p)^\beta$, $p < 1$ is equal to an infinite series which is convergent. In order to extend our result (34) to include positive non–integral values of β , we may define two–dimensional non–integral function on Δ_2 as convergent infinite series and then by subjecting it to the entropy properties given in (a_1), (a_2) and (a_3) exactly as above, we shall derive what may be called as *"two–dimensional non–integral algebraic entropy"* given by

$$(35) \qquad \begin{cases} \mathfrak{B}(p) = \dfrac{p^\beta + (1-p)^\beta - 1}{2^{1-\beta} - 1}, \\[2mm] \beta > 0 \text{ and non–integer.} \end{cases}$$

Remark 2   In order to overcome the problem for $\beta = 1$, we shall take the limiting case as follows:

$$(36) \qquad \lim_{\beta \to 1} \mathfrak{B}(p) = - p \log_2 p - (1-p) \log_2 (1-p)$$

which is the Shannon entropy. This is a transcendental entropy, studied elsewhere in this work.

Now defining a two–dimensional complete probability algebraic function as a real, finite or convergent infinite series on Δ_2, and which satisfies the entropy–properties as given in (a_1), (a_2) and (a_3), we derive uniquely from it, by combining (34), (35) and (36), the quantity

$$(37) \qquad \mathcal{B}(p) = \frac{p^\beta + (1-p)^\beta - 1}{2^{1-\beta} - 1}, \, \beta > 0, \, \beta \neq 1$$

which we shall call as the "*two-dimensional algebraic entropy*". The extension to higher dimension is straightforward.

The approach outlined above enables us to derive measures of information from various mathematical functions subjected to desired properties. Studies of properties and some applications of polynomial entropy may be found elsewhere in this monograph. For an application in relation to one of the latest works of Menges, see Behara, Kofler and Menges (1978). For characterization of polynomial entropy using functional equations, see Behara and Nath (1974). An account of geometric entropy or, in particular, parabolic entropy, (the idea of polynomial entropy is derived from parabolic entropy, the methods of derivation are, however, different) based on Behara and Nath (1973) may be found in Guiasu (1977).

2.1.1 Characterization of Polynomial Entropy

In this section, we consider a functional equation connected with polynomial entropy $^{\beta}h_n \equiv h_n$, $n = 2,3,4,...$, defined as

(1)
$$\begin{cases} {}^{\beta}h_n(p_1,p_2,...,p_n) = \dfrac{\sum\limits_{i=1}^{n} p_i^{\beta} - 1}{c}, \\ c = 2^{1-\beta} - 1, \quad \beta > 0, \beta \neq 1. \end{cases}$$

It is easily seen that (1) can be written as

(2)
$$^{\beta}h_n(p_1,p_2,...,p_n) = \sum_{i=1}^{n} {}^{\beta}z(p_i)$$

where $Z(p) \equiv {}^{\beta}z(p): [0,1] \to \mathbb{R}$ is defined as

(3)
$$\begin{cases} {}^{\beta}z(p) = \dfrac{p^{\beta} - p}{c}, \quad p \in [0,1], \\ c = 2^{1-\beta} - 1, \beta > 0, \beta \neq 1, 0^{\beta} = 0. \end{cases}$$

Let $(p_1,p_2,...,p_n) \in \Delta_n$ and $(q_1,q_2,...,q_m) \in \Delta_m$ be any two arbitrarily chosen discrete probability distributions and let

$$(p_1q_1,p_1q_2,...,p_1q_m;...;p_nq_1,p_nq_2,...,p_nq_m) \in \Delta_{nm}$$

denote their direct product. Then it can be easily verified that Z satisfies functional equation

$$(4) \quad \begin{bmatrix} \sum_{i=1}^{n} \sum_{j=1}^{m} g(p_i q_j) = \sum_{i=1}^{n} g(p_i) + \sum_{j=1}^{m} g(q_j) \\ +c \sum_{i=1}^{n} g(p_i) \sum_{j=1}^{n} g(q_j), \; c = 2^{1-\beta} - 1. \end{bmatrix}$$

Also, from (3), it is obvious that

$$(5) \qquad \beta_z(\tfrac{1}{2}) = 1/2.$$

The following theorem regarding (4) is due to Behara and Nath (1971):

Theorem 1 *The necessary and sufficient condition that a real-valued continuous function* g: $[0,1] \to \mathbb{R}$, $g(\tfrac{1}{2}) = 1/2$, *satisfies the functional equation* (4) *for all positive integers* m *and* n *is that* g = β_z *where* β_z *is of the form* (3).

Proof The sufficiency part is a simple verification, of course, with c = $2^{1-\beta} - 1$. Now we prove that the condition is necessary. Let us write

$$n = u - r + 1, \quad m = v - s + 1$$

where u, r, v and s are positive integers and $1 \leq r \leq u$, $1 \leq s \leq v$. Let us choose,

$$p_i = 1/u, \quad i = 1,2,...,u-r; \quad p_{u-r+1} = r/u$$
$$q_j = 1/v, \quad j = 1,2,...,v-s; \quad q_{v-s+1} = s/v.$$

It is clear that $p_1+p_2+..+p_n = q_1+q_2+ +q_m = 1$. Substitution in (4) yields

(6)
$$\begin{cases} (u-r)(v-s) g(\frac{1}{uv}) + (u-r) g(\frac{s}{uv}) + (v-s) g(\frac{r}{uv}) + g(\frac{rs}{uv}) \\[2mm] = [(u-r) g(\frac{1}{u}) + g(\frac{r}{u})] + [(v-s) g(\frac{1}{v}) + [g(\frac{s}{v})] \\[2mm] +c [(u-r) g(\frac{1}{u}) + g(\frac{r}{u})] [(v-s) g(\frac{1}{v}) + g(\frac{s}{v})]. \end{cases}$$

Let us now choose $r = s = 1$. Then from (6), we obtain,

(7)
$$uv \, g(\tfrac{1}{uv}) = u \, g(\tfrac{1}{u}) + v \, g(\tfrac{1}{v}) + c \, [u \, g(\tfrac{1}{u})] \, [v \, g(\tfrac{1}{v})].$$

Let us define $\psi: [1,\infty) \to \mathbb{R}$ as

(8)
$$\psi(t) = 1 + t \, g(1/t), \quad t \in [1,\infty).$$

Then (7) reduces to

(9)
$$\psi(uv) = \psi(u). \, \psi(v), \quad u,v \text{ positive integers.}$$

The continuity of g implies that ψ is a continuous function of $x \in [1,\infty)$. Hence, by Theorem 3 on page 41 of Aczel (1966), the only continuous solution of (9) are of the form

(10) $\qquad \psi(x) \equiv 0$ and $\psi(x) = x^k$, k arbitrary real

In the case $\psi(x) \equiv 0$, we get

$$g(x) = -x/c, \quad c = 2^{1-\beta}, \quad x \in (0,1], \quad \beta \neq 1.$$

Putting $x = 1/2$ and using the fact that $g(\frac{1}{2}) = 1/2$, we get $2^{1-\beta} - 1 = 1$ implies $2^{1-\beta} = 0$ which is impossible because, β is a real number different from unity. Hence corresponding to $\psi(x) \equiv 0$, we do not get any solution of functional equation (4) satisfying the boundary condition $g(\frac{1}{2}) = 1/2$.

Corresponding to $\beta f(x) = x^k$, we get

(11) $\qquad \begin{cases} g(x) = \dfrac{x^{1-k}(1-x^k)}{c}, \ c = 2^{1-\beta} - 1, \\[2mm] x \in (0,1), \ \beta \neq 1, \ k \text{ arbitrary real.} \end{cases}$

The condition $g(\frac{1}{2}) = 1/2$ gives $k = 1 - \beta$ so that

(12) $\qquad \begin{cases} g(x) = \dfrac{x^\beta - x}{c}, \ c = 2^{1-\beta} - 1, \\[2mm] \beta \neq 1, \ x \in (0,1]. \end{cases}$

By continuity and the convention $0^r = 0$, r real, g is given by (12) for all $x \in (0,1]$. Then, we have

(13)
$$\begin{cases} g(x) = \dfrac{x^\beta - x}{c}, \, c = 2^{1-\beta} - 1, \\ x \in [0,1], \, \beta \neq 1. \end{cases}$$

This completes the proof of Theorem 1.

Kannappan (1974) discussed the functional equation

(14)
$$\begin{cases} \displaystyle\sum_{i=1}^{n} \sum_{j=1}^{m} g(p_i q_j) \\ \\ = \displaystyle\sum_{i=1}^{n} g(p_i) + \sum_{j=1}^{m} g(q_j) + c \sum_{i=1}^{n} g(p_i) \sum_{j=1}^{m} g(q_j), \\ \\ 0 \neq c \in \mathbb{R}, \, p_i \geq 0, \, q_j \geq 0, \, \Sigma p_i = \Sigma q_j = 1; \\ \\ i = 1, 2, .., n; \, j = 1, 2, .., m; \, m, n = 1, 2, 3, ... \end{cases}$$

assuming g to be a continuous real–valued function with domain [0,1]. It is obvious that (14) is a general form of (4). Note that in (14), c is a non–zero real number. The following theorem is due to Kannappan (1974).

Theorem 2 *If* g: [0,1] → ℝ *is a continuous function which satisfies* (14) *for all positive integers* m *and* n, *then* g *is either of the form*

(15)
$$g(x) = - x/c, \, x \in [0,1], \, c \neq 0$$

or

$$(16) \qquad g(x) = \frac{x^{1-k} - x}{c}, \ x \in [0,1], \ k \in \mathbb{R},$$

with the convention $0^r = 0$, *for all* $r \in \mathbb{R}$.

Proof Let $n = m = 1$. Then $p_1 = q_1 = 1$. Consequently, $g(1) \ [1 + c \ g(1)] = 0$ which means that $g(1) = 0$ or $g(1) = -1/c$ Suppose,

$$(17) \qquad g(1) = -1/c.$$

Let us choose $n = 1$ and $q_j = 1/m$, $j = 1,2,...,m$; $p_1 = 1$. Then (14) yields

$$(18) \qquad g(1/m) = -1/cm, \ m = 1,2,3,...$$

Let $n = 2$, $m = 1$. Set $p_1, p_2 = 0$, $q_1 = 1$. Then, using (17) and (14), we obtain

$$(19) \qquad g(0) = 0.$$

Let m and n be any arbitrary positive integers. Choose $m \leq n$ and set

$$(20) \qquad p_1 = m/n; \ p_2 = p_3 = ... = p_{n-m+1} = 1/n.$$

Then, making substitution in (14) and using (18), we get $g(m/n) = -m/nc$. In other words, we have proved that

$g(x) = - x/c$ for all positive rationals in $(0,1]$. By the continuity of q, this result can be extended to all real numbers in $[0,1]$ and thus we get (15).

Now suppose that

(21) $g(1) = 0.$

Let us define a mapping f: $[1,\infty) \to \mathbb{R}$ as

(22) $f(x) = 1 + c\, g(1/x), \quad x \geq 1.$

Putting $p_i = 1/n$, $q_j = 1/m$, $i = 1,2,...,n;\ j = 1,2,...,m$, and making use of (22) and (14), we get

(23) $f(n\, m) = f(n)\, f(m), \quad m,n = 1,2,3,...$

Now, let $m \leq n$ and choose p_i's according to (20) with $q_j = 1/m$, $j = 1,2,...,m$. Then, making use of (22) and (14), we obtain

(24) $f(m)\, f(n/m) = f(n),\ m,n = 1,2,3,...;\ m \leq n.$

We prove that for no positive integer n, $f(n)$ equals zero. If possible, let there exist a positive integer m_0 such that $f(m_0) = 0$. Then, choosing $m = m_0$ in (24), it follows that $f(n) = 0$ for all positive integers $n \geq m_0$. Now, let us choose $1 < n \leq m_0$. Then, we can always find a positive integer ℓ such that $n^{\ell} > m_0$. On the other hand, from (23) we also have $[f(n)]^{\ell} = f(n^{\ell})$ and since $n^{\ell} > m_0$, therefore, $f(n^{\ell}) = 0$. and, consequently, $[f(n)]^{\ell} = 0$ which implies $f(n) = 0$. Thus, we get $f(n) = 0$ for all positive integers n. Consequently, (22) yields

$$g(1/n) = -1/cn.$$

In particular, $g(1) = -1/c$ which is a contradiction to the fact that $g(1) = 0$. Hence, we conclude that, for no positive integer n, $g(n) = 0$. Now from (24) we obtain

$$(25) \qquad f(n/m) = f(n)/f(m), \quad 1 \leq m \leq n.$$

From (23) and (25), it follows that for all rationals $r \geq 1$, $s \geq 1$,

$$(26) \qquad f(r\,s) = f(r)\,f(s), \quad r \geq 1 \text{ and } s \geq 1.$$

The continuity of q implies the continuity of f in $[1, \infty)$. Consequently, (26) leads to

$$(27) \qquad f(x\,y) = f(x)\,f(y), \quad x \geq 1, y \geq 1.$$

The continuous solutions of (27) are of the forms

$$(28) \qquad \begin{cases} f(x) \equiv 0, \quad f(x) = x^{\nu}, \\ \nu \text{ an arbitrary constant.} \end{cases}$$

The case $f(x) \equiv 0$ yields

$$g(x) = -x/c \text{ which implies } g(1) = -1/c,$$

a contradiction to (21). The case $f(x) = x^{\nu}$ leads to

$$g(x) = \frac{x^{1-k} - x}{c}, \quad x \in (0,1]$$

This completes the proof of Theorem 2.

Remark 1. If we assume $g(\frac{1}{2}) = 1/2$, then solutions (15) and (16) reduce respectively to

(29) $g(x) = x, \quad x \in [0,1]$

and

(30) $\begin{cases} g(x) = \frac{x^\beta - x}{c}, \quad c = 2^{1-\beta} - 1, \\ x \in [0,1], \ \beta \neq 1 \end{cases}$

In the case of (29), $\Sigma \, g(p_i) = 1$ and hence $\Sigma \, g(p_i)$ no longer represents an entropy. However, in the case of (30), we have

$$\sum_{i=1}^{n} g(p_i) = \left[\sum_{i=1}^{n} p_i^\beta - 1 \right] \Big/ \left[2^{1-\beta} - 1 \right], \ \beta \neq 1.$$

Kannappan (1979, unpublished) has given a lemma which enables us to solve a large number of functional equations. Below, we give that Lemma and then solve (14) to find its continuous solutions.

Lemma 1   *Let f: [0,1] → ℝ be continuous. Then f is a solution of the functional equation*

$$(31) \qquad \sum_{i=1}^{n} f(x_i) = c \quad with \ (x_1, x_2, ..., x_n) \ \epsilon \ \Delta_n$$

for fixed n ≥ 3, c, *a constant if and only if*

$$(32) \qquad f(x) = ax + b \quad with \ a + nb = c,$$

where a *and* b *are constants.*

Proof   If f is of the form (32), then obviously f satisfies (31). Conversely, let f be a solution of (31).

Letting $x_1 = u$, $x_2 = v$, $x_3 = 1-u-v$, $x_4 = 0 = ... = x_n$, (31) takes the form

$$(33) \qquad \begin{cases} f(u) + f(v) + f(1-u-v) = d, \\ u,v,u+v \ \epsilon \ [0,1] \ , where \ d \ is \ a \ constant. \end{cases}$$

For v = 0, (33) is $f(u) + f(0) + f(1-u) = d$, so that (33) can be rewritten as ,

$$f(u) + f(v) = f(u+v) + f(0).$$

Since f is continuous, f is of the form

$$f(x) = ax + b.$$

Then f given by (32) is a solution provided a+nb = c.

Corollary 1 *If* c = 0 *in* (31), f *continuous, then the solution of* (31) *is of the form*

$$f(x) = ax + b \quad with \quad a + nb = 0.$$

Corollary 2 *Suppose* (31) *holds for* n = 2 *and* n = 3, *with* f *continuous. Then*

$$f(x) + f(1-x) = c \quad and \, f(x) = b\,(3x-1) + c\,x,$$

where b *is any arbitrary constant. That is,* b = 0, *so that, the solution of* (31), *when* (31) *holds for* n = 2 *and* n *is* f(x) = c x.

Corollary 3 *If* f *satisfies* (31) *for all* n ≥ 2 *with* f *continuous, then* f(x) = c x.

This follows easily from Corollary 2.

Solution of (14) using Lemma 1 of Kannappan (1979, unpublished) is given below. In order to solve (14) for the general case, first let us solve (14) when n = 3 = m, that is,

(34)
$$\begin{bmatrix} \sum_{i=1}^{3} \sum_{j=1}^{3} g(p_i q_j) \\ = \sum_{i=1}^{3} g(p_i) + \sum_{j=1}^{3} g(p_j) + c \sum_{i=1}^{3} g(p_i) \sum_{i=1}^{3} g(p_j) \end{bmatrix}$$

where $c \neq 0$, $g: [0,1] \to \mathbb{R}$, is continuous with $(p_1, p_2, p_3) \in \Delta_3$ and $(q_1, q_2, q_3) \in \Delta_3$. In what follows, all Σ are for $i=1$ to 3 and for $j=1$ to 3, as the case may be.

Since $g(p) = 0$ is a solution of (34), in the following we seek non–trivial solution of (34).

For fixed q_1, q_2, q_3, define

(35)
$$h(p) = \sum_{j=1}^{3} g(pq_j) - g(p) - p \sum_{j=1}^{3} g(q_j) - c\, g(p) \sum_{j=1}^{3} g(q_j)$$

for $p \in [0,1]$. Then h is continuous and satisfies (31) for $n = 3$ so that by Lemma 1,

(36)
$$h(p) = a\,(3p - 1), \quad p \in [0,1],$$

where a is a constant dependent on q_1, q_2, q_3.

From (35) and (36), we get

(37)
$$\begin{bmatrix} h(0) = -a = g(0)\,[2 - c\,\Sigma\,g(q_j)] \\ h(1) = 2a = -\,g(1)\,[1 + c\,\Sigma\,g(q_j)], \end{bmatrix}$$

so that

(38) $\qquad c \sum g(q_j) [g(1) + 2 g(0)] = 4 g(0) - g(1).$

Suppose $g(1) + 2 g(0) \neq 0$, then $\sum g(q_j) = \text{constant} = b$ (say). By Lemma 1, $g(q)$ is of the form

(39) $\qquad g(q) = aq + d,$

where a, d are constants with $a + 3d = b$. Now, g given by (39) is a solution of (34) provided

(40) $\qquad c(a+3d)^2 + a - 3d = 0.$

Now suppose $g(1) + 2 g(0) = 0$. Then from (38), it follows that, $g(0) = 0 = g(1)$. Now, (35), (36) and (37) yield

(41) $\qquad \sum g(pq_j) - g(p) - p \sum g(q_j) - c g(p) \sum g(q_j) = 0.$

For fixed p, defining

$$\kappa(q) = g(pq) - q g(p) - p g(q) - c g(p) g(q)$$

for $q \in [0,1]$, it is easy to see that, κ is continuous and satisfies (31) for $n = 3$ and that

$$\kappa(q) = \alpha (3q - 1), \quad q \in [0,1]$$

where α is a function of p. But,

$$\kappa(0) = -\alpha = 0 \quad (\text{since } g(0) = 0).$$

Thus,

(42)
$$\begin{cases} g(pq) = q\,g(p) + p\,g(q) + c\,g(p)\,g(q), \\ \text{with } p,q \in [0,1]. \end{cases}$$

By taking

$$\ell(p) = 1 + c\,\frac{g(p)}{p}, \quad \text{for } p \in (0,1],$$

(42) can be rewritten as,

$$\ell(pq) = \ell(p) + \ell(q), \quad \text{for } p,q \in (0,1],$$

with ℓ continuous. Thus,

$$\ell(p) \equiv 0 \quad \text{or} \quad \ell(p) = p^{\beta-1} \text{ for some } \beta, \, p \in (0,1].$$

We notice that $\ell(p) = 0$ leads to

$$g(p) = -p/c \quad \text{for } p \in (0,1]$$

[which is part of the solution given by (38) satisfying (40) with $d = 0$, $a = -1/c$] which is not possible, since $g(1) = -1/c \neq 0$. Now $\ell(p) = p^{\beta}$ leads to

(43)
$$g(p) = \frac{p\,(p^{\beta-1} - 1)}{c}, \quad \text{for } p \in (0,1].$$

Since $g(1) = 0$, $\beta \neq 1$. Otherwise $g \equiv 0$.

Since $g(0) = 0$, (43) holds also for $p = 0$ when $\beta \neq 0$, that is,

(44) $$g(p) = \frac{p^\beta - p}{c}, \text{ for } p \in [0,1], \text{ with } \beta \neq 1,0.$$

Since $g = 0$ is a solution of (34), (44) is a solution of (34) for all $\beta = 1$

For $\beta = 0$, $g(p) = (1 - p)/c$ which is part of the solution of (39) with $a = -1/c$, $d = 1/c$. Thus (44) is a solution of (34) for all β with $0^\beta = 0$, $1^\beta = 1$. Hence, we proved the following theorem.

Theorem 3. *Let* $g: [0,1] \to \mathbb{R}$ *be continuous. Then* f *satisfies the functional equation* (34) *iff* g *is given either by* (39) *with the condition* (40) *or by* (44).

Corollary 4. *Suppose g is continuous and satisfies* (14) *for all integers m, n $\geq$ 2. Then g is given by*

(44) *or* $g(x) = -x/c.$

Proof Evidently g given by (44) satisfies (14) irrespective of m and n.

But g given by (39) with the condition (40) is a solution of (14) for all m, n only if $d = 0$ and $a = -1/c$.

2.1.2 Characterization of Polynomial Entropy without prior β

One of the advantages in dealing with functional equations (14) of 2.1.1, rather than (4) of 2.1.1, is that it enables us to characterize nonadditive entropy βh_n axiomatically without assuming the prior existence of the parameter. Our next task is to give another way of characterizing βh_n axiomatically without assuming the prior existence of the parameter β.

Let E be any event which occurs with positive probability $p \,\epsilon\, (0,1]$. How much information do we obtain when we are told that an event E has occurred with positive probability $p \,\epsilon\, (0,1]$? We assume that the information yielded by the occurrence of E is a function of the probability with which E occurs. Let $F: (0,1] \rightarrow \mathbb{R}$ such that $F(p)$ denotes the amount of information obtained when E occurs with probability $p \,\epsilon\, (0,1]$.

Definition 1.   *A function* $F: (0,1] \rightarrow \mathbb{R}$ *is called an information function if it satisfies the following properties:*
    (a)   *F is a continuous function of* $p \,\epsilon\, (0,1]$,
    (b) $F(\tfrac{1}{2}) = 1, \; F(1) = 0.$
    (c) $F(pq) = \phi[F(p), F(q)],$ *where ϕ is a polynomial of its arguments.*

The following theorem is due to Behara and Nath (1974).

Theorem 1   *Let F be a real–valued function defined on* (0,1] *and satisfy* (a), (b) *and* (c). *Then F is given by*

(1) $$F(p) = \left[\frac{1 - p^{\beta-1}}{1 - 2^{1-\beta}}\right], p \, \epsilon \, (0,1], \beta \neq 1$$

or

$$F(p) = -\log_2 p, \, p \, \epsilon \, (0,1], \, \beta = 1.$$

Proof Let

(2) $$F(pq) = \phi\Big[\, F(p), F(q) \,\Big] = F(p) \, \square \, F(q).$$

Then, it can be easily seen that the operation ' $\square$ ' is commutative and associative. Let ϕ be a polynomial of degree n in $F(p)$ and of degree m in $F(q)$. Because of symmetry, m = n. Then by the associativity, $n^2 = n$ so that n = 0,1. If n = 0, then $F(p) =$ constant which is a contradiction to (b). So, only n = 1 is possible. Then, because of symmetry, we must have

(3) $$\phi(F(p), F(q)) = a \, F(p)F(q) + b \, F(p) + b \, F(q) + c$$

where $ac = b^2 - b$. Hence

(4) $\qquad F(pq) = a\,F(p)F(q) + b\,F(p) + b\,F(q) + c.$

Let $a = 0$. Then, $b = 1$ and (4) reduces to

(5) $\qquad F(pq) = F(p) + F(q) + c$

Putting

(6) $\qquad g(p) = F(p) + c,$

we have (5) reducing to

(7) $\qquad g(pq) = g(p) + g(q),\ p\epsilon(0.1],\ q\epsilon(0,1].$

By (a) and (6), g is a continuous function of $p \epsilon (0,1]$. Hence, the continuous solutions of (7) are of the form $g(p) = K \log_2 p$ where K is an arbitrary constant. Then, $F(p) = \kappa \log_\beta p = c$. By (b) $F(\tfrac{1}{2}) = 1$ and $F(1) = 0$. Hence, $c = 0, \kappa = -1$ so that

(8) $\qquad F(p) = -\log_\beta p,\ \beta = 1.$

If $a \neq 0$, then the substitution

(9) $\qquad h(p) = a\,F(p) + b,\ a \neq 0.$

which reduces (4) to Cauchy's equation

(10) $\qquad h(pq) = h(p) h(q), p,q\in(0,1].$

continuous solutions of (10) are of the form $h(p) \equiv 0$ and $h(p) = p^{\beta-1}$, $\beta \in \mathbb{R} = (-\infty,+\infty)$. If $h(p) \equiv 0$, then $F(p) = -\dfrac{b}{a}$, a constant which is a contradiction to (b). If $h(p) = p^{\beta-1}$, then we cannot allow $\beta = 1$ because this will mean that $h(p) = 1$ and, consequently, $F(p) = \dfrac{1-b}{a}$ which is again a contradiction to (b). With $h(p) = p^{\beta-1}$, $\beta \neq 1$, we get

$$F(p) = \frac{p^{\beta-1} - b}{a}, \ a \neq 0, \ p\in(0,1].$$

By (b), it can be seen that $b = 1$, $a = 2^{1-\beta} - 1$, $\beta \neq 1$. Hence,

(11) $\qquad F(p) = \dfrac{p^{\beta-1} - 1}{2^{\beta-1} - 1}, \ \beta \neq 1, \ p\in(0,1].$

We can combine (8) and (11) to get (1). This proves Theorem 1.

Remark 1 The assumptions (a) and (b) are self—explanatory. However, assumption (c) needs some justification. It is customary to assume the additive nature of information, that is,

(12) $\qquad F(pq) = F(p) + F(q), \ p\in(0,1], \ q\in(0,1].$

The RHS in (12) is a particular case of (c) when we choose $\phi(x,\bar{y}) = x + y$. Obviously, ϕ is a symmetric polynomial of its arguments. If the RHS in (12) is taken as an arbitrary polynomial in $F(p)$ and $F(q)$, then it is natural to expect some more measures of information and this is precisely the justification to assume (c). Indeed, we have seen that for $\beta \neq 1$, $F(p)$ is a nonadditive measure of information.

We have already mentioned above the operation '□' is both commutative and associative. If we put $F(1) = e$, then

$$(13) \qquad F(p) = F(p) \,\square\, F(1) = F(1) \,\square\, F(p)$$

Also, from (c), the range of ϕ is the same as that of F. Since F is a non–constant function, therefore, the range of ϕ cannot be a singleton set. In fact, the functional equation (2) admits of at least one non–constant continuous solution provided the range of F forms a commutative monoid under the operation '□' and the identity of the monoid is $F(1) = e$.

From (1), it is easily seen that $F(p) \geq 0$. Thus the range of F is $\mathbb{R}^+ = \{x: x \geq 0\}$ and $(\mathbb{R}^+, \square)$ is a commutative monoid under the operation '□'. Let $U = (0,1]$. Then, it is easily seen that $(U, \cdot)$ is a commutative multiplicative monoid under ordinary multiplication '·' and with identity 1. Thus, the functions $F(p)$, β, constitute the set Δ of all mappings from $(U, \cdot)$ into $(\mathbb{R}^+, \cdot)$ satisfying (a), (b) and (c).

From information–theoretic point of view, $F(p)$ can be interpreted as the entropy of order β of a generalized singleton distribution (p), $p \in (0,1]$. The conditions (a), (b) and (c) mentioned in Definition 1 are enough to characterize it. From (1), it is now clear that the entropy of a generalized singleton probability distribution is not always additive. In order to study the entropy of a generalized singleton probability distribution, a detailed study of $F(t)$, $t \in (0,1]$, is therefore necessary.

From (a), it is obvious that the continuity of F has not been assumed at $p = 0$. Hence, nothing can be said, in general, regarding the continuity of $F(p)$ at $p = 0$. But, from the form of $F(p)$ in (1), one can easily see that $F(p)$ has a defined value even at $p = 0$ for all $\beta > 1$ and, moreover, it is continuous at $p=0$ for all $\beta > 1$. Let us define βF^*: $[0,1] \to \mathbb{R}$, only for $\beta > 1$, as follows:

(14)
$$\begin{cases} \beta F^*(p) = \beta F(p), \ p \in (0,1] \\[2mm] \beta F^*(0) = \lim_{p \to 0} \beta F(p), \ p = 0 \end{cases}$$

Clearly, the new function βF^* is also continuous at $p = 0$. The continuity of an information function is, indeed, an intuitive requirement. $\beta F^*(0) = \lim_{p \to 0} \beta F(p)$ means the amount of information obtained when we are told that an event with probability zero has occurred. Is this amount of information finite or infinite? It seems difficult to decide this question as we notice that

$$\beta F^*(0) = \lim_{p \to 0} \beta F(p) = 2; \ \beta = 2$$

$$\beta F^*(0) = \lim_{p \to 0} \beta F(p) = 4/3, \ \beta = 3$$

$$\lim_{p \to 0} \beta F^*(p) = \infty, \ 0 \le \beta \le 1.$$

Now we discuss some properties of $\beta F(p)$.

P_1 It is easy to see that $\beta F(p) \ge 0$ and $\lim_{p \to 0} \beta F(p)$ lies between 0 and $+\infty$.

P_2 $p \to F(p)$, $p \epsilon (0,1]$, is a strictly monotonically decreasing function of p.

P_3 $\beta F(p)$ is a convex function of p for $0 \le \beta \le 2$ and a concave function of p for $2 < \beta < \infty$.

P_4 βF is a strictly subadditive function of p, that is, $\beta F(p_1+p_2) < \beta F(p_1) + \beta F(p_2)$.

P_5 βF satisfies functional equation (15)

(15) $\begin{cases} \beta F(pq) = \beta F(p) + \beta F(q) + (2^{1-\beta} - 1) \beta F(p) \beta F(q) \\ p \ \epsilon \ (0.1], \ q \ \epsilon \ (0,1], \ \beta \ \epsilon \ \mathbb{R}. \end{cases}$

In particular,

$$^\beta F(pq) \leq {}^\beta F(p) + {}^\beta F(q), \, p, \, q\epsilon(0,1], \, 1 < \beta < \infty$$
$$^\beta F(pq) \geq {}^\beta F(p) + {}^\beta F(q), \, p, \, p\epsilon(0,1], \, 0 < \beta < 1$$
$$^\beta F(pq) = {}^\beta F(p) + {}^\beta F(q), \, p, \, q\epsilon(0,1], \, \beta = 1$$

$P_6 \, (a_1)$ $\quad$ $^0F(p) = \dfrac{1-p}{p}$, $p\epsilon(0,1]$. Due to the fact that $p \, \epsilon \, (0,1]$, we need to consider only that part of the branch which commences from the point $(1,0)$ and becomes asymptotic to y–axis. The asymptotes of the hyperbola are the lines $x = 0$ and $y = -1$.

From (15), it is obvious that F satisfies the functional equation

(16) $\quad \begin{bmatrix} {}^0F(pq) = {}^0F(p) + {}^0F(q) + {}^0F(p) \, {}^0F(q), \\ p\epsilon(0,1], .q\epsilon(0,1]. \end{bmatrix}$

In addition to it, ^0F also satisfies the equation

(17) $\quad {}^0F(p) = 2p^2 - 3p + 1/p, \, p \, \epsilon \, (0,1].$

(a_2) $\quad$ $^1F(p) = -\log_2 p, \, p \, \epsilon \, (0,1].$

Both ^0F and ^1F pass through the points $(1,0)$ and $(\frac{1}{2},1)$ and as $p \rightarrow 0$, both become asymptotic to their y–axis. It can easily be seen that ^1F is a strictly monotonically decreasing function of p ϵ (0,1].

(a_3) $^2F(p) = 2(1-p)$, p ϵ (0,1]. In this case, we have $^2F^*(p) = 2(1-p)$, p ϵ (0,1]. It can be easily seen that the graph of $^2F^*$ is a straight line passing through the points (1,0) and (0,2). It intersects both ^0F and ^1F only at (1,0) and($\frac{1}{2}$,1). It is obvious that

(18) $^2F^*(p) + {}^3F^*(1-p) = 2$, p ϵ [0,1].

Let

(19) $g(p) = \frac{1}{2} \, {}^2F^*(p)$, p ϵ [0,1].

Then (18) reduces to

(20) $g(p) + g(1-p) = 1$, pϵ[0,1].

which is a functional equation in one variable. Equation (24) has infinitely many continuous solutions and they can be obtained by choosing an arbitrary continuous graph joining the points ($\frac{1}{2}$,$\frac{1}{2}$) and (0,1) and then extending this continuous function from ($\frac{1}{2}$,$\frac{1}{2}$) to (0,1) by defining

$$g(p) = 1-g(1-p). \quad p\epsilon[0,\tfrac{1}{2}].$$

(a_4) $^3F(p) = \frac{4}{3}(1-p^2)$, p$\epsilon$(0,1].

Consequently, $^3F^*(p) = \frac{4}{3}(1-p^2)$, $p \in [0,1]$. It can be easily seen that the graph of $^3F^*$ is a parabola with vertex $(0,4/3)$ and focus $(0,1)$.

(a₅) For positive integral values of $\beta \geq 2$,
$^\beta F(p)$ is a polynomial of degree $(\beta-1)$ in p.

(a₆) $\beta \to {}^\beta F$ is a continuous function such that
$\beta_1 < \beta_2$ implies $^{\beta_2}F(p) \leq {}^{\beta_1}F(p)$, $p \in (0,\frac{1}{2}]$
$\beta_1 < \beta_2$ implies $^{\beta_1}F(p) \leq {}^{\beta_2}F(p)$, $p \in [\frac{1}{2},1]$.

(a₇) (i) $\beta \to {}^\beta F(p) \in [1,2]$, $\beta \in [2,\infty]$, $p \in [0,\frac{1}{2}]$.
(ii) $\beta \to {}^\beta F(p) \in [0,1]$, $\beta \in [0,\infty]$, $p \in [\frac{1}{2},1]$
(iii) It is only in the region $p \in (0,\frac{1}{2}]$ that
$^\beta F(p)$, for all $\beta \in [0,1]$, becomes infinite as $p \to 0$.
(iv) $\lim_{\beta \to \infty} {}^\beta F(p) = 1$, $p \in [0,1]$.

(a₈) $^\beta F^*(p) \geq 1$, $\beta \geq 2$, $p \in [0,\frac{1}{2}]$
$^\beta F^*(p) \leq 1$, $\beta \geq 2$, $p \in [\frac{1}{2},1]$.

Let us consider the Euclidean metric $d(x,y) = \{[(x_1-x_2)^2 + (y_1-y_2)^2]$ where $x = (x_1,x_2)$ and $y = (y_1,y_2)$. Then, it can be easily seen that, with respect to this metric, the sets

$$^\beta E = \{(p,{}^\beta F(p)), p \in [0,1]\}, \beta \in G = [2,\infty]$$

are both connected as well as compact. Obviously, for any $S \subset G$, $\cap \ \beta E \neq \phi$. Hence,

$$\mathscr{E} \equiv \underset{\beta \epsilon G}{\cup} \ \beta E \text{ is connected but not compact.}$$

Let D_1 denote the set of all points lying inside and on the triangle with vertices $(0,2)$, $(0,1)$, $(\frac{1}{2},1)$ and D_2 denote the triangle with vertices $(\frac{1}{2},1)$, $(0,1)$ and $(1,1)$. Obviously, D_1 and D_2 are both connected and compact sets. Moreover,

$$(21) \qquad \mathscr{E} = \underset{\beta \epsilon G}{\cup} \ \beta E \subset (D_1 \cup D_2) \equiv \mathscr{D}.$$

The sets D_1 and D_2 can in fact be transformed into each other because to each $(x^*,y^*) \in D_2$, there corresponds $(x,y) \in D_1$ such that

$$(22) \qquad x^* = 1 - x \qquad \text{and} \qquad y^* = 2 - y.$$

Also
$$(23) \qquad \mathscr{D} \backslash \ \mathscr{E} = \{(1,y) : 0 < y < 1\}$$
and

$$(24) \qquad \overline{\mathscr{E}} = \overline{\underset{\beta \epsilon G}{\cup} \ \beta E} = D_1 \cup D_2$$

where $\mathscr{D} \backslash \ \mathscr{E}$ denotes the set of all those points which belong to

$D_1 \cup D_2$ but not to $\mathscr{E}$, and $\overline{\mathscr{E}}$ denotes the closure of $\mathscr{E}$.

$\qquad$ (a_9) $\quad$ (i) $^2F(p) = 2p \ ^0F(p)$, $p \in (0,1]$.

$$(\text{ii}) \quad \begin{cases} F(p) = \left[\dfrac{1 - 2^{2-\beta}}{1 - 2^{1-\beta}}\right] \beta^{-1}F(p) + c\, p^{\beta-1}\, {}^0F(p). \\[2ex] c = (1 - 2^{1-\beta}),\ \beta > 2. \end{cases}$$

(a_{10}) $\qquad$ ${}^\beta F(p) \neq {}^\beta F(1-p)$, $p \in (0,1)$, except when $p = 1/2$. This clearly shows that ${}^\beta F$ lacks symmetry. However, it is possible to construct some symmetric functions with the aid of ${}^\beta F$.

For instance, the functions Ψ_β defined as

$$(25) \qquad \Psi_\beta(p) = {}^\beta F(p) + {}^\beta F(1-p),\ p \in (0,1),\ \beta \in [0,\infty)$$

are symmetric in $(0,1)$ in the sense that $\Psi_\beta(p) = \Psi_\beta(1-p)$, $p \in (0,1)$. Also, Ψ_β is monotonic decreasing function of p, $0 < p < 1/2$ and monotonic increasing function of p, $1/2 \le p \le 1$. For $0 < \beta \le 1$, $\Psi_\beta(0)$ and $\Psi_\beta(1)$ are not defined. However, for $\beta > 1$, the function Ψ_β can be extended with the aid of ${}^\beta F^*$ so that the new function, so obtained is defined at 0 and 1 and it takes the same value at 0 and 1 in order that it is also symmetric in $[0,1]$.

The function Ψ_β is not necessarily a polynomial of degree $(\beta-1)$ for positive integral values of β. Rather, $\Psi_\beta(p)$ is a polynomial of degree $(\beta-1)$ for positive odd integral values of β and of degree $\beta-2$ for positive even integral values of β. In particular, $\Psi_2(p) = 2$, a straight line and

$$\Psi_3(p) = \frac{4}{3}(1 + 2p - 2p^2), \text{ a parabola.}$$

(a₁₁) $^\beta F(p)$ contains only one parameter β. Let us define a two–parameter family of functions $^{\beta_1\beta_2}F : (0,1] \to \mathbb{R}$ as

(26)
$$\begin{cases} ^{\beta_1\beta_2}F(p) = \dfrac{p^{\beta_2^{-1}} - p^{\beta_1^{-1}}}{2^{1-\beta_2} - 2^{1-\beta_1}}, \\ \beta_1 \neq \beta_2; \ p \in (0,1], \ \beta_1 \geq 0, \ \beta_2 \geq 0. \end{cases}$$

Obviously, $^{\beta_1}{}^1F(p) = F(p)$ and, moreover,

(27)
$$^{\beta_1\beta_2}F(p) = \frac{(1-2^{1-\beta_1})\ ^{\beta_1}F(p) - (1-2^{1-\beta_2})\ ^{\beta_2}F(p)}{(1-2^{1-\beta_1}) - (1-2^{1-\beta_2})}$$

It can be easily verified that $^{\beta_1\beta_2}F(p) \geq 0$, $^{\beta_1\beta_2}F(\frac{1}{2}) = 1$ and, which, in the limiting case for $\beta_2 \to \beta_1 (\equiv \beta^*)$ becomes

(28)
$$^{\beta^*}\zeta(p) = -2^{\beta^*-1}\ p^{\beta^*-1} \log_2 p, \ \beta^* \geq 0, \ p\in(0,1].$$

Evidently, $^1\zeta(p) = {}^1F(p)$. This shows that ^1F can be generalized not only to $^\beta F$ but also to $\beta^*\zeta$ which is also non–additive for $\beta^* \neq 1$.

The functions $^{\beta_1\beta_2}F$ satisfy the functional equations

(29)
$$\begin{cases} \beta_1\beta_2 F(pq) = q^{\beta_1-1}\ \beta_1\beta_2 F(p) + p^{\beta_2-1}\ \beta_1\beta_2 F(q), \\ (p,q \in (0,1]),\ \beta_1 \neq \beta_2 \ . \end{cases}$$

whose most general solutions are

(30)
$$\beta_1\beta_2 F(p) = \lambda(p^{\beta_1-1} - p^{\beta_2-1}),\ \beta_1 \neq \beta_2 \ .$$

where λ is an arbitrary constant.

Let $(p_1,p_2,...,p_n) \in \Delta_n$ be any complete probability distribution. If we restrict to $\beta > 0,\ \beta \neq 1$, then

(31)
$$\beta_h{}_n(p_1,p_2,..,p_n) = \frac{\sum\limits_{i=1}^{n} p_i^{\beta} - 1}{2^{1-\beta} - 1},\ \beta > 0,\ \beta \neq 1.$$

denotes β—entropy $\beta_h{}_n(p_1,p_2,...,p_n)$ introduced earlier. In a similar way, if we restrict to $\beta_1 > 0,\ \beta_2 > 0,\ \beta_1 \neq \beta_2$, then

$$\sum_{i=1}^{n} p_i\ \beta_1\beta_2 F(p_i) := \beta_1\beta_2 h_n(p_1,p_2,...,p_n)$$

denotes another entropy, where

(32)
$$\begin{cases} \beta_1\beta_2 h_n(p_1,p_2,...,p_n) \\ \\ = \dfrac{\sum\limits_{i=1}^{n} p_i^{\beta_1} - \sum\limits_{i=1}^{n} p_i^{\beta_2}}{2^{1-\beta_1} - 2^{1-\beta_2}},\ \beta_1 \neq \beta_2,\ \beta_1 > 0,\ \beta_2 > 0, \end{cases}$$

which, in the limiting case when $\beta_2 \to \beta_1 (\equiv \beta^*)$ reduces to

$$(33) \qquad \beta^* h_n(p_1,...,p_n) = -2\beta^{*-1} \sum_{i=1}^{n} p_i^{\beta^*} \log_2 p_i, \; \beta^* > 0$$

The measure given in (32) will be called the $\beta_1\beta_2-$ entropy whereas the measure in (33) will be called β^*-entropy, Both of these entropies were proposed in Behara and Nath (1974). The β_1 β_2-entropy is an algebraic entropy whereas the β_1,β_2-entropy and β^*-entropy are obviously nonadditive entropies. It is clear that, for $\beta_2 = 1$, (32) reduces to $\beta h_n(p_1,p_2,...,p_n)$. Also, for $\beta^* = 1$, (33) reduces to the Shannon entropy. Both (32) and (33) can be characterized, simultaneously by means of a functional equation which, of course, involves the parameters β_1 and β_2 explicitly. According to our view, this is a disadvantage with our characterization but we have not yet been successful in characterizing (32) and (33) without assuming the prior existence of the parameters β_1 and β_2.

The following result is due to Behara and Nath (1974).

Theorem 2 *The necessary and sufficient condition that a continuous real-valued function* g: $[0,1] \to \mathbb{R}$, $g(\tfrac{1}{2}) = 1/2$ *satisfies the functional equation*

(34)

$$
\begin{cases}
\sum_{i=1}^{n} \sum_{j=1}^{m} g(p_i q_j) \\
= \left[\sum_{j=1}^{m} q_j^{\beta_1} \right] \left[\sum_{i=1}^{n} g(p_i) \right] + \left[\sum_{i=1}^{n} p_i^{\beta_2} \right] \left[\sum_{j=1}^{m} g(p_j) \right], \\
\beta_1 > 0, \ \beta_2 > 0, \ 0^{\beta_1} = 0^{\beta_2} = 0, \\
p_i \geq 0, \ q_j \geq 0, \ i=1,2,\dots,n; \ j = 1,2,\dots,m; \\
\sum_{i=1}^{n} p_i = 1 = \sum_{j=1}^{m} q_j
\end{cases}
$$

for all positive integers m *and* n *is that* $g = \beta_1 \beta_2 f$ *where*

(35) $\qquad \beta_1 \beta_2 \, f(p)$

$$
\begin{cases}
= 0, \ p = 0,1 \\
= \dfrac{p^{\beta_1} - p^{\beta_2}}{2^{1-\beta_1} - 2^{1-\beta_2}}, \ p\epsilon(0,1), \ \beta_1 \neq \beta_2 \\
= -2^{\beta^* -1} p^{\beta^*} \log_2 p, \ p\epsilon(0,1), \\
\beta_1 = \beta_2 = \beta^*,
\end{cases}
$$

Proof The sufficiency part is a simple verification. To prove the necessary part, we proceed as follows: By the application of Lemma 1 of 2.1.1, we immediately get the functional equation

(36)
$$
\begin{cases}
g(xy) = y^{\beta_1} g(x) + x^{\beta_2} g(y), \\
\beta_1 > 0, \ \beta_2 > 0, \ x \in [0,1], \ y \in [0,1]
\end{cases}
$$

Put $x = y = 0$. Since $0^{\beta_1} = 0^{\beta_2} = 0$, therefore, we get

$g(0) = 0$. Setting $x = y = 1$ we get $g(1) = 0$. Thus $g(0) = g(1) = 0$. Hence, it is enough to consider the functional equation

$$(37) \qquad \begin{cases} g(xy) = y^{\beta_1} g(x) + x^{\beta_2} g(y), \\ \beta > 0, \ x \in (0,1), \ y \in (0,1). \end{cases}$$

Let $\beta_1 \neq \beta_2$. Then, (37) gives

$$(38) \qquad \begin{cases} y^{\beta_1} g(x) + x^{\beta_2} g(y) = x^{\beta_1} g(y) + y^{\beta_2} g(x), \\ x,y \in (0,1), \end{cases}$$

from which it follows that $g(x) = \lambda(x^{\beta_1} - x^{\beta_2})$, λ an arbitrary constant. Since $g(\frac{1}{2}) = (1/2)$, therefore,

$$\lambda = (2^1\beta_1 - 2^1\beta_2)^{-1}$$

and we get

$$g(x) = \frac{x^{\beta_1} - x^{\beta_2}}{2^1\beta_1 - 2^1\beta_2}.$$

Now, we discuss the case when $\beta_1 = \beta_2 = \beta^*$ In this case, (37) reduces to

$$(39) \qquad \begin{cases} g(xy) = y^{\beta^*} g(x) + x^{\beta^*} g(y), \\ x, y \in (0,1), \ \beta^* > 0. \end{cases}$$

which can be written in the form

(40)
$$\begin{cases} \dfrac{g(xy)}{(xy)^{\beta^*}} = \dfrac{g(x)}{x^{\beta^*}} + \dfrac{g(y)}{y^{\beta^*}}, \\[2mm] \beta^* > 0, \; x,y \in (0,1). \end{cases}$$

Putting $\xi_\beta^*(x) = \dfrac{g(x)}{x^{\beta^*}}$, (40) reduces to

(41)
$$\begin{cases} \xi_\beta^*(xy) = \xi_\beta^*(x) + \xi_\beta^*(y), \\[2mm] \beta^* > 0, \; x,y \in (0,1). \end{cases}$$

The continuity of ξ implies that ξ_β^* is continuous in $(0,1)$. Hence $\xi_\beta^*(x) = \lambda \log_2 x$ where λ is an arbitrary constant. Thus, $g(x) = \lambda x^{\beta^*} \log_2 x$. But $g(\tfrac{1}{2}) = 1/2$. Hence $\lambda = -2^{\beta^*} - 1$ so that $g(x) = -2^{\beta^* - 1} x^{\beta^*} \log_2 x$, $x \in (0,1)$. This completes the proof of Theorem 1.

2.1.3 Properties of Polynomial Entropy

In this section, we give some properties of ${}^{\beta}h_n$, $\beta > 0$, $\beta \neq 1$.

P_1 ${}^{\beta}h_n$ is a *continuous* function of its arguments.

P$_2$ $^\beta h_n$ is a *symmetric* function of its arguments.

P$_3$ For all positive integers m,n, and for all probability distributions

$$\begin{cases} (p_1,p_2,...,p_n) \in \Delta_n, \\ (q_1,q_2,...,q_m) \in \Delta_m, \end{cases}$$

(1)

$$\begin{cases} ^\beta h_{nm}(p_1q_1,p_2q_2,...,p_1q_m,...; \; p_nq_1,p_nq_2,..,p_nq_m) \\[2mm] = \; ^\beta h_n(p_1,p_2,...p_n) + \, ^\beta h_m(q_1,q_2,...,q_m) \\[2mm] + \; (2^{1-\beta} - 1) \, ^\beta h_n(p_1,p_2,...,p_n) \, ^\beta h_m(q_1,q_2,...,q_m) \end{cases}$$

Equation (1) is called *additivity of degree β*.

P$_4$ For all positive integers n 3, with $p_{n-1} + p_n = 0$,

$$(p_1,p_2,...,p_{n-2}, \; p_{n-1},p_n) \in \Delta_n$$

(2)

$$\begin{cases} ^\beta h_n(p_1,p_2,...,p_{n-2},p_{n-1},p_n) \\[2mm] = \; ^\beta h_{n-1}(p_1,p_2,...,p_{n-2},p_{n-1} + p_n) \\[2mm] + \; (p_{n-1} + p_n) \; ^\beta h_2\left[\dfrac{p_{n-1}}{p_{n-1}+p_n} \, , \, \dfrac{p_n}{p_{n-1}+p_n}\right] \end{cases}$$

Equation (2) is called *recursivity of degree β*.

P_5 For all positive integers n and m,

(3)
$$\begin{cases} \beta h_{nm}(r_{11},...,r_{1m};r_{21},...,r_{2m};...;r_{n1},...r_{nm}) \\[2mm] = \beta h_n(p_1,p_2,...,p_n) + \sum_{i=1}^{n} p_i^{\beta}\, \beta h_m(r_{1/i},r_{2/i},...,r_{m/i}), \\[2mm] \sum_{i=1}^{n} \sum_{j=1}^{m} r_{ij} = 1, \end{cases}$$

Equation (3) is called *strong additivity of degree β*.

P_6 βh_n is subadditive for all $\beta > 1$, that is,

(4)
$$\begin{cases} \beta h_{nm}(r_{11},...,r_{1m};\, r_{21},...,r_{2m};\, ...;\, r_{n1},..,r_{nm}) \\[2mm] \leq \beta h_n\left[\sum_{i=1}^{n} t_{i1},\ \sum_{i=1}^{n} r_{i2},...,\ \sum_{i=1}^{n} r_{im}\right] \\[2mm] + \beta h_m\left[\sum_{j=1}^{m} r_{1j},\ \sum_{j=1}^{m} r_{2j},...,\ \sum_{j=1}^{m} r_{nj}\right]. \end{cases}$$

P_7 For all positive integers $n \geq 1$,

(5)
$$\begin{cases} \beta h_{n+1}(p_1,p_2,...,p_n,0) \quad = \quad \beta h_n(p_1,p_2,...p_n), \\[2mm] (p_1,p_2,...,p_n) \in \Delta_n \end{cases}$$

P_8 $p \to \beta h_2(p,1-p)$ is *strictly monotonically increasing function of* $p \in (0,\tfrac{1}{2})$ *and strictly monotonically decreasing function of* $p \in (\tfrac{1}{2},1)$.

An interesting feature of polynomial entropy $^{\beta}h_n$ is that it is very closely connected with the Rényi entropy $^{\alpha}H_n$. One can easily see that, for $\alpha = \beta$,

$$^{\beta}H_n(p_1,...,p_n) \quad \begin{cases} = (1-\beta)^{-1}\log_2[2^{1-\beta}\,^{\beta}h_n(p_1,..,p_n) - 1], \\ \\ (p_1, p_2,..., p_n) \in \Delta_n. \end{cases}$$

Note that, polynomial entropy possesses some useful properties which the Rényi entropy does not possess. For example; for $\alpha > 0$, $\alpha \neq 1$, the Rényi entropy is not subadditive whereas polynomial entropy is $^{\beta}h_n$ is *subadditive*. The subadditive and superadditive properties of various entropies are studied in Behara and Nath (submitted), " On Classification of Entropies: Subadditivity and Pseudo–Subadditivity."

2.2   NONPOLYNOMIAL ALGEBRAIC ENTROPY

We have studied polynomial entropies under algebraic entropy previously. In what follows, we shall study an entropy which can be represented by the graph of an algebraic but nonpolynomial function. Such an entropy, therefore, belongs to the class of nonpolynomial algebraic entropies and has been studied by Behara and Chawla (1974).

For a complete probability distribution $P_n = (p_1, p_2, .., p_n)$ consider the function

(1)
$$\left[\begin{array}{l} F(P_n) \equiv F(p_1,...,p_n) = \left[\sum_{k=1}^{n} p_k^{1/\gamma} \right]^{\gamma}, \\ \gamma > 0, \; \gamma \neq 1. \end{array} \right.$$

Following Hardy et al (1952), we have

(2)
$$\left[\begin{array}{l} F(\lambda P_n + (1-\lambda)Q_n) \geq \lambda F(P_n) + (1-\lambda)F(Q_n), 0 < \gamma < 1 \\ F(\lambda P_n + (1-\lambda)Q_n) \leq \lambda F(P_n) + (1-\lambda)F(Q_n), \; \gamma > 1. \end{array} \right.$$

where $0 < \lambda < 1$ and P_n, Q_n are any two complete probability distributions. The function given in (1), therefore, is concave for $\gamma < 1$ and convex for $0 < \gamma < 1$.

(3)
$$\left[\begin{array}{l} {}^{\gamma}h_n(p_1,...,p_n) = c_1 \left[\sum_{k=1}^{n} p_k^{1/\gamma} \right]^{\gamma} + c_2, \\ c_1 \text{ and } c_2 \text{ are arbitrary constants.} \end{array} \right.$$

If the above function (3) were to represent an entropy measure, we should have, intuitively, for two–dimensional case,

(4)
$$\qquad {}^{\gamma}h_2(\tfrac{1}{2},\tfrac{1}{2}) = 1 \qquad \text{and} \qquad {}^{\gamma}h_2(1,0) = 0.$$

By using (4) in the two–dimensional case of (3), we have

(5)
$$\qquad c_1 + c_2 = 0$$
and

(6) $\qquad c_1[(\tfrac{1}{2})^{\gamma} + (\tfrac{1}{2})^{\gamma}]^{\gamma} + c_2 = 1$

which is equivalent to

(7) $\qquad c_1 \, 2^{\gamma-1} + c_2 = 1.$

Solving (5) and (7), we get

(8) $\qquad c_1 = -c_2 = \dfrac{1}{2^{\gamma-1} - 1}.$

Thus, (3) may be written as

(9) $\qquad {}^{\gamma}h_n(p_1,..,p_n) = \dfrac{1 - \left[\sum\limits_{k=1}^{n} p_k^{\,1/\gamma}\right]^{\gamma}}{1 - 2^{\gamma-1}}, \; \gamma \neq 1, \, \gamma > 0.$

As $c_1 > 0$ or < 0 according as $\gamma > 1$ or $0 < \gamma < 1$, the function ${}^{\gamma}h_n$, $\gamma > 0$, $\gamma \neq 1$ given in (9) is concave. We shall call the function (9) as the γ–entropy. As noted above, the γ–entropy is a nonpolynomial algebraic entropy.

2.2.1 Characterization of the Gamma–Entropy.

Let $(p_1, p_2, ..., p_n) \in \Delta_n$. The Shannon entropy $H_n(p_1, p_2, ..., p_n)$ may be regarded as

$$(1) \quad \begin{cases} H_n(p_1, p_2, \ldots, p_n) \\ = \inf_{(q_1, q_2, \ldots, q_n) \in \Delta_n} -\sum_{i=1}^{n} p_i \log_2 q_i \end{cases}$$

This is obvious from Shannon inequality. In fact, (1) may be regarded as a definition [Arimoto (1971)]. This definition can be used to define other entropies.

Let $f: (0,1] \to \mathbb{R}$ be a real-valued continuous function satisfying the following axioms:

(a_1) f is a continuous function of $p \in (0,1]$.

(a_2) $f(\tfrac{1}{2}) = j$

(a_3) f satisfies the functional equation.

$$(2) \quad \begin{cases} f(xy) = f(x) + f(y) + (2^{\gamma-1} - 1) f(y), \\ 0 < x \le 1, 0 < y \le 1, \gamma > 0, \gamma \ne 1. \end{cases}$$

We prove the following theorem.

Theorem 1 *If* $f: (0,1) \to \mathbb{R}$ *satisfies* $(a_1),(a_2)$ *and* (a_3), *then* $f = {}^{\gamma}f$ *where*

$$(3) \quad {}^{\gamma}f(x) = \frac{x^{\gamma} - 1}{2^{\gamma-1} - 1}, \quad \gamma > 0, \gamma \ne 1.$$

Proof Let $\phi: (0,1] \to \mathbb{R}$ be defined as

$$(4) \quad \phi(x) = 1 + (2^{\gamma-1} - 1) f(x), \quad x \in (0,1].$$

Then, (2) reduces to

(5) $\phi(xy) = \phi(x)\,\phi(y)$, $x \in (0,1]$, $y \in (0,1]$.

The continuity of f implies the continuity of ϕ. Hence, the continuous solutions of (5) are of the form

(6) $\phi(x) = 0$ and $\phi(x) = x\,k$, k an arbitrary constant.

We do not allow $k = 0$ because if $k = 0$, then $\phi(x) = 1$ and then f will be an identically vanishing function which is a contradiction to (2). Hence, only $k \neq 0$ is possible. We may write $k = 1-\gamma$. Because $\gamma \neq 1$, therefore, $k \neq 0$.

The solution $\phi(x) = 0$ gives

$$^{\gamma}f(x) = \frac{1}{1-2^{1-\gamma}}, \; x \in (0,1].$$

Put $x = 1/2$. Using the fact that $f(\tfrac{1}{2}) = 1/2$, we get $2 = 1-2^{1-\gamma}$ implying $2^{1-\gamma} = -1$ which is an absurdity because $2^{1-\gamma}$ is always positive. Hence, the only admissible form of ϕ is $\phi(x) = x^{1-\gamma}$, $\gamma \neq 1$. Consequently, $f(x) = {}^{\gamma}f(x)$ where

$$^{\gamma}f(x) = \frac{1 - x^{1-\gamma}}{1 - 2^{\gamma-1}}$$

This completes the proof of Theorem 1.

Following the definition of Arimoto (1971), let us define

$$^\gamma h_n(p_1, p_2, ..., p_n) = \inf - \sum_{i=1}^{n} p_i \left[\frac{1 - q^{1-\gamma}}{1 - 2^{\gamma-1}} \right],$$

infimum being taken with respect to all $(q_1, q_2, ..., q_n) \in \Delta_n$. It can be easily seen, by the use of Holders's inequality, that

$$(7) \qquad \begin{bmatrix} ^\gamma h_n(p_1, p_2, ..., p_n) = \dfrac{1 - \left[\sum_{i=1}^{n} (p_i)^{1/\gamma} \right]^\gamma}{1 - 2^{\gamma-1}}, \\ \gamma > 0, \ \gamma \neq 1. \end{bmatrix}$$

The entropy $^\gamma h_n(p_1, p_2, ..., p_n)$, called the γ-entropy, is due to Behara and Chawla (1974). It is nonadditive and an algebraic function. For no value of γ, $^\gamma h_n$ is a polynomial of its arguments.

Corollary 1 *For $\gamma = 1$, axiom (a_3) reduces to*

$$(8) \qquad f(xy) = f(x) + f(y)$$

and its solution is

$$(9) \qquad f(x) = c \log x.$$

Using axiom (a_2), we obtain

(10) $$f(x) = -\log x$$

Now,

(11) $${}^{1}h_n = \inf - \sum_{i=1}^{n} p_i \log x_i$$

where inf is taken with respect to all $(x_1,...,x_m) \in \Delta_n$. it follows easily that

(12) $${}^{1}h_n(p_1,...,p_n) = -\sum_{i=1}^{n} p_i \log p_i.$$

Thus the Shannon entropy happens to be a member of the γ-entropy. It is also a limiting case of ${}^{\gamma}h_n$ as seen below:

$$\lim_{\gamma \to 1} {}^{\gamma}h_n(p_1,...,p_n)$$

$$= \lim_{\gamma \to 1} \frac{1 - \left[\sum_{i=1}^{n} p_i^{1/\gamma}\right]^{\gamma}}{1 - 2^{\gamma-1}}$$

$$= \lim_{\gamma \to 1} \frac{\dfrac{d}{dr}\left[\sum_{i=1}^{n} p_i^{1/\gamma}\right]^{\gamma}}{\dfrac{d}{dr}\left[2^{\gamma-1}\right]}$$

$$= \lim_{\gamma \to 1} \frac{\left[\sum_{i=1}^{n} p_i^{1/\gamma}\right]^{1/\gamma}}{2^{\gamma-1} \ln 2} \kappa$$

where κ is given by

$$\kappa = \ln \sum_{i=1}^{n}(p_i)^{1/\gamma} - \frac{1}{\gamma}\left[\sum_{i=1}^{n}(p_i)^{1/\gamma}\ln p_i\right]\Big/\left[\sum_{i=1}^{n}(p_i)^{1/\gamma}\right]$$

Therefore, we have finally

(13) $$\lim_{\gamma \to 1} {}^{\gamma}h_n(p_1, p_2, ..., p_n) = -\sum_{i=1}^{n} p_i \log p_i.$$

2.2.2 Properties of the Gamma–Entropy

The γ–entropy ${}^{\gamma}h_n$ has a number of interesting algebraic and analytic properties, some of which are given below:

P_1 ${}^{\gamma}h_n$ is a *continuous* function of its arguments.

P_2 ${}^{\gamma}h_n$ is *expansible*.

P_3 ${}^{\gamma}h_2(\frac{1}{2}, \frac{1}{2}) = 1$.

P_4 ${}^{\gamma}h_n$ is a *symmetric* function of its arguments.

P_5 $$\lim_{\gamma \to 0^+} {}^{\gamma}h_n(p_1, p_2, ..., p_n) = 2\left[1 - \max_{1 \le i \le n} p_i\right].$$

Proof   Let $p_n \ge p_i$, $i = 1, 2, ..., n$ and $p_m = p_i$ for all values of i. Then,

$$\lim_{\gamma \to 0^+} {}^{\gamma}h_n(p_1,\ldots,p_n)$$

$$
\begin{cases}
= \lim_{\gamma \to 0^+} \dfrac{1 - \left[\sum\limits_{i=1}^{n}(p_i)^{1/\gamma}\right]^{\gamma}}{1 - 2^{\gamma-1}} \\[30pt]
= \lim_{\gamma \to 0^+} \dfrac{1 - p_m\left[\sum\limits_{i=1}^{n} p_i(p_i/p_m)^{1/\gamma}\right]^{\gamma}}{1 - 2^{\gamma-1}} \\[30pt]
= 2\,[1 - p_m] \\[10pt]
= 2\,[1 - \max_{1 \le i \le n} p_i].
\end{cases}
$$

P_6 $\qquad 0 \le {}^{\gamma}h_n(p_1,\ldots,p_n) \le \dfrac{1 - n^{\gamma-1}}{1 - 2^{\gamma-1}}$

Proof $\qquad$ Case 1: $\gamma < 1$.

$$\sum_{i=1}^{n}(p_i)^{1/\gamma} \le 1$$

$$
\begin{cases}
\Rightarrow \left[\sum\limits_{i=1}^{n}(p_i)^{1/\gamma}\right]^{\gamma} \le 1 \\[25pt]
\Rightarrow 1 - \left[\sum\limits_{i=1}^{n}(p_i)^{1/\gamma}\right]^{\gamma} \ge 0 \\[25pt]
\Rightarrow \dfrac{1 - \left[\sum\limits_{i=1}^{n}(p_i)^{1/\gamma}\right]^{\gamma}}{1 - 2^{\gamma-1}} \ge 0
\end{cases}
$$

Case 2: $\gamma > 1$.

$$\left[\sum_{i=1}^{n}(p_i)^{1/\gamma}\right]^{\gamma} \geq 1 \qquad \Rightarrow 1 - \left[\sum_{i=1}^{n}(p_i)^{1/\gamma}\right]^{\gamma} \leq 0$$

$$\Rightarrow \frac{1 - \left[\sum_{i=1}^{n}(p_i)^{1/\gamma}\right]^{\gamma}}{1 - 2^{\gamma-1}} \geq 0$$

Thus, in both the cases, $\gamma < 1$ and $\gamma > 1$, $^{\gamma}h_n(p_1,...,p_n) \geq 0$. Now, to prove

$$^{\gamma}h_n \geq \frac{1 - n^{\gamma-1}}{1 - 2^{\gamma-1}}$$

we use

$$^{\gamma}h_n \begin{cases} = \inf_{(x_1,...,x_n) \in \Delta_n} \sum_{i=1}^{n} p_i\, f(x_i) \\ \leq \sum_{i=1}^{n} p_i\, f(1/n) \\ = f(1/n). \end{cases}$$

Applying (3) of 2.2.1 we have,

$$f(1/n) = \frac{1 - n^{\gamma-1}}{1 - 2^{\gamma-1}}.$$

P_7 For all positive integers m and n,

$$^{\gamma}h_{nm}(p_1q_1,..,p_1q_m;p_2q_1,..,p_2q_m;..;p_nq_1,..,p_nq_m)$$

$$
\begin{cases}
= {}^{\gamma}h_n(p_1,p_1,..,p_n) + {}^{\gamma}h_m(q_1,q_2,...,q_m) \\
+ (2^{\gamma-1}-1)\ {}^{\gamma}h_m(p_1,..,p_n)\ {}^{\gamma}h_m(q_1,..,q_m).
\end{cases}
$$

which may be written, for brevity,

$$
{}^{\gamma}h_{nm} = {}^{\gamma}h_n + {}^{\gamma}h_m + (2^{\gamma-1})\ {}^{\gamma}h_n\ {}^{\gamma}h_m.
$$

From the definition of γ-entropy, we have

$$
{}^{\gamma}h_{nm} = \frac{1 - \left[\sum_{=1}^{n} \sum_{j=1}^{m} (p_iq_j)^{1/\gamma}\right]^{\gamma}}{1 - 2^{\gamma-1}}
$$

$$
= \frac{1 - \left[\sum_{i=1}^{n} \sum_{j=1}^{m} (p_i)^{1/\gamma}(q_j)^{1/\gamma}\right]^{\gamma}}{1 - 2^{\gamma-1}}
$$

$$
= \frac{1 - \left[\sum_{i=1}^{n}(p_i)^{1/\gamma}\right]^{\gamma}\left[\sum_{j=1}^{m}(q_j)^{1/\gamma}\right]^{\gamma}}{1 - 2^{\gamma-1}}
$$

$$
= \frac{1}{1-2^{\gamma-1}}\left\{-\left[1-\left[\sum_{i=1}^{n}(p_i)^{1/\gamma}\right]^{\gamma}\right]\left[1-\left[\sum_{j=1}^{m}(q_j)^{1/\gamma}\right]^{\gamma}\right] \right.
$$
$$
\left. + \left[1-\left[\sum_{i=1}^{n}(p_i)^{1/\gamma}\right]^{\gamma}\right] + \left[1-\left[\sum_{j=1}^{m}(q)^{1/\gamma}\right]^{\gamma}\right]\right\}
$$

$$
= h_n^{(\gamma)} + h_m^{(\gamma)} - (1 - 2^{\gamma-1})\ h_n^{(\gamma)}\ h_m^{(\gamma)}.
$$

P8   For $(p_1,...,p_n) \in \Delta_n$, $(q_1,...,q_m) \in \Delta_m, n < m$, then

$$
{}^{\gamma}h_n(p_1,...,p_n) \leq {}^{\gamma}h_m(q_1,...,p_m).
$$

One major difference between the β-entropy and the γ-entropy is that the former admits a sum–representation of the type (2) of 2.1.1 whereas the latter does not admit of such a sum–representation. Therefore, the associated functional equation used to characterize the β-entropy cannot be used to characterize the γ-entropy.

2.2.3 Conditional Gamma–Entropy

Writing $P_n = (p_1, p_2, ..., p_n)$ and, $Q_m = (q_1, q_2, ..., q_m)$ and

$$R_{nm} = P_n{}^*Q_m = (r_{11}, ..., r_{1m}; r_{21}, ..., r_{2m}; ...; r_{n1}, ..., r_{nm})$$

for probability distributions P_n, Q_m and the joint probability distribution $P_n{}^*Q_m$ respectively, then the conditional γ-entropy of P_n with respect to Q_m is given by

(1)
$$
\begin{cases}
{}^{\gamma}h_{n,m}(P_n/Q_m) \\[2mm]
\sum\limits_{j=1}^{m} q_j \ {}^{\gamma}h_n(r_{1/j}, r_{2/j}, ..., r_{n/j}) \\[2mm]
= \dfrac{1}{1-2^{\gamma-1}} \sum\limits_{j=1}^{m} q_j \left[1 - \sum\limits_{i=1}^{n} (r_{i/j})^{1/\gamma} \right]^{\gamma} \\[2mm]
\text{where } \gamma_{i/j} = r_{ij}/q_j
\end{cases}
$$

If P_n and Q_m are independent, that is, if $r_{ij} = p_i q_j$, $i = 1,...,n$, $j = 1,...,m$, then

$$(2) \qquad {}^\gamma h_{n,m} (P_n/Q_m) = {}^\gamma h_n (P_n) = \frac{1 - \left[\sum\limits_{i=1}^{n} (p_i)^{1/\gamma} \right]^\gamma}{1 - 2^{\gamma-1}}$$

If $P_{n_1} = (p_1,...,p_{n_1})$ and $P_{n_2} = (p_1,...,p_{n_2})$ are two probability distributions such that $n_1 \leq n_2$, then

$$(3) \qquad {}^\gamma h_{n_1,m} (P_{n_1}/Q_m) \leq {}^\gamma h_{n_2,m} (P_{n_2}/Q_m)$$

and

$$ {}^\gamma h_{m,n_1}(Q_m/P_{n_1}) \geq {}^\gamma h_{m,n_2}(Q_m/P_{n_2}) $$

where $Q_m = (q_1,...,q_m)$ any probability distribution.

2.3 TRANSCENDENTAL ENTROPIES

So far, we have been able to investigate only two new classes of trigonometric entropies in the class of nonadditive transcendental entropies. In what follows, we shall describe the most recent results on trigonometric entropies due to Behara and Chorneyko (accepted).

Let $\Delta_n = \{(p_1,..,p_n); p_k > 0; k=1,..n; \Sigma\, p_k=1; n=2,3, ..\}$

be the set of all finite discrete n–component probability

distributions with non–negative elements. Let $\mathfrak{C}_n$ be the class of functions $f_n: \Delta_n \rightarrow \mathbb{R}$, for all positive integers n, satisfy the following axioms [Behara (1985)], called the fundamental axioms of entropy:

(a_1) $f_n(1,0,0,...,0) = 0$

(a_2) $f_n(\frac{1}{n},...,\frac{1}{n})$ is maximum.

(a_3) $f_n(p_1,p_2,...,p_n) \quad = \quad f_n(p_{k(1)},p_{k(2)},...,p_{k(n)})$,
        i.e., $f_n(p_1,p_2,...,p_n)$ is permutation symmetric for all positive integers.

Any function $f_n \in \mathfrak{C}_n$ is a measure of information known as entropy. However, each entropy measure satisfies some more properties in addition to (a_1), (a_2) and (a_3), which will distinguish its nature from the other. We note that the following entropies belong to the above class $\mathfrak{C}_n$.

I   Shannon entropy [Shannon (1948)]. For all $P \in \Delta_n$

$$H(P) = -\sum_{k=1}^{n} p_k \log_2 p_k, \ \sum_{k=1}^{n} p_k = 1, \ p_k \geq 0.$$

II   Rényi entropy [Rényi(1960)]. For all $P \in \Delta_n$

$$^{\alpha}H_n(P) = (1-\alpha)^{-1} \log_2 \sum_{k=1}^{n} p_k^{\alpha}, \ \alpha > 0, \ \alpha \neq 1.$$

III   Algebraic entropy [Behara(1985)]. For all $P \in \Delta_n$

$$\beta h_n(P) = \frac{\sum\limits_{k=1}^{n} p_k^{\beta} - 1}{2^{1-\beta} - 1}, \beta > 0, \beta \neq 1.$$

In particular, ${}^2h_2(p) = 2 \, [1 - \sum\limits_{k=1}^{2} p_k^2]$ under the name "*parabolic entropy*" was studied in Behara and Nath (1973). See also Guiasu(1977). But in addition to the above entropies, there are several other entropies which belong to $\mathfrak{C}_n$. In this work, we shall study a new class of entropies called trigonometric entropies since these have been derived from some trigonometric functions belonging to the class $\mathfrak{C}_n$.

2.3.1 Trigonometric Entropies

Let

(1) $$t(p_k) = \frac{\sin \Pi \, p_k}{2 \, p_k}, \, 0 \leq p_k \leq 1, \, \sum\limits_{k=1}^{n} p_k = 1$$

be the self–information function due to the probability p_k of the occurrence of the kth event of an experiment. The function $T_n \, (P)$ is the average amount of uncertainty with the experiment, where

(2) $$T_n(P) = \sum\limits_{k=1}^{n} p_k \, t(p_k) = \sum\limits_{k=1}^{n} \frac{\sin \Pi \, p_k}{2}, \, P \, \epsilon \, \Delta_n.$$

The above entropy $T_n(P)$ satisfies the fundamental axioms

(a_1), (a_2),(a_3) of an information measure. These axioms are sufficient to develop an information measure but any such entropy may satisfy some additional properties. We shall study the properties of $T_n(P)$.

P_1. $T_n(1,0,0,...,0) = 0$

P_2. $T_n(p_1,p_2,...,p_n)$ is maximum only if
$p_1 = p_2 = ... = p_n$

P_3. $T_n(p_1,p_2,...,p_n)$ is *permutational symmetric* function of its arguments i.e.,
$T_n(p_1,p_2,...,p_n) = T_n(p_{k(1)}, p_{k(2)},...,p_{k(n)})$.

P_4. $T_n(p_1,p_2,...,p_n)$ is a *continuous* function of p_k, $k = 1,2,...,n$

P_5 $T_n(P) \geq 0$, $P \in \Delta_n$

P_6. $T_{n+1}(p_1,p_2,...,p_n,0) = T_n(p_1,p_2,...,p_n)$

P_7.   The graph of T_2 $(p,1-p)$ is *symmetric* about $p = \frac{1}{2}$. It is *monotonically increasing* from $0 \leq p \leq \frac{1}{2}$. It attains maximum value 1 at $p = \frac{1}{2}$ and minimum value 0 at $p = 0$ or 1.

P_8.   (a) Let $E_i = (0,0,...,1,...,0,...,0) \in \Delta_n$ be the n–component vector with the ith component 1, and the other components 0. For any $P = E_i$, $Q \in \Delta_n$ or for any $Q = E_i$ and $P \in \Delta_n$

$$\begin{cases} \text{(b)} \quad T_n(P*Q) = T_n(P) + T_n(Q) \\ \text{(c)} \quad T_n(P*Q) \leq T_n(P) + T_n(Q), \\ P,Q \in \Delta_n, \; P \neq E_1, \; Q \neq E_i \end{cases}$$

where

$$P * Q = (p_1q_1, p_1q_2, ..., p_1q_n; ...; p_nq_1, p_nq_2, ..., p_nq_n)$$

P_9. *Recurrence* relation: For $P \in \Delta_n$,

$$T_n(p_1, p_2, ..., p_n)$$
$$\begin{cases} = T_{n-1}(p_1+p_2, p_3, ..., p_n) + T_2(p_1, p_2) \\ - T_1(p_1) \sqrt{[1-T_2^2(p_2)]} - T_2(p_2) \sqrt{[1-T_1^2(p_1)]} \end{cases}$$

The proofs of the properties are obvious).

2.3.2 Comparison of Shannon and Trigonometric Entropies

Properties P_1–P_6 of trigonometric entropy holds for the Shannon entropy.

$P_7{}'$ The graph of the Shannon entropy for $n = 2$, i.e., $H_2(p, 1-p)$, is similar to $T_2(p, 1-p)$ except for its rate of increase between 0 and $\frac{1}{2}$.

P_8' $H_n(P*Q) \leq H_n(P) + H(Q)$, where equality holds only when P and Q are statistically independent.

P_9' $H_n(p_1, p_2, ..., p_n)$

$$\begin{bmatrix} = H_{n-1}(p_1 + p_2, p_3, ..., p_n) \\ + (p_1 + p_2) H_2 \left[\dfrac{p_1}{p_1 + p_2}, \dfrac{p_2}{p_1 + p_2} \right] \end{bmatrix}$$

Remark 1. A simple generalization of the trigonometric entropy (2) is given below:

$$T_n^{\alpha}(P) = \sum_{k=1}^{n} \frac{\sin^{\alpha} \prod p_k}{2}, P \epsilon \Delta_n, \alpha > 0.$$

PART THREE

CODING THEORY

3.0 INTRODUCTION

Although Golay(1949) and Hamming (1950) may be regarded as the foundation of modern coding theory, the idea of codes was inherent in Bose (1939). Coding theory is studied under (a) probabilistic coding theory and (b) algebraic coding theory. Algebraic coding theory originated from probabilistic coding theory, the fundamental theorem of which is known as the Shannon theorem of information theory. Interestingly, historians claim that, even though included in the initial work of R.W. Hamming earlier, the Shannon theorem made its appearance in Shannon (1948).

Shannon theorem guarantees the existence of codes whereas algebraic coding theory supplies methods for construction of codes, and encoding and decoding of such codes. Codes are transmitted over channels which are described by probabilistic schemes. Ideally, the transmission of codes should be made at high rate with as small error as possible. Here, the capacity of a channel comes under consideration.

We shall confine ourselves to the study of probabilistic coding theory in this part of the monograph. In particular, coding theory for Shannon, Rényi and polynomial entropies will be studied here. Pioneering works such as Campbell (1965) in probabilistic coding theory paved the way to a vast and yet an unattempted area filled with rich and useful research resources.

3.1 CODING THEORY FOR SHANNON ENTROPY

We shall now study the applications of various measures
of entropy in coding theory. Let us assume that the messages
to be transmitted can be written down in terms of the values
$x_1, x_2, ..., x_n$ taken by a random variable X with probabilities

$$p_1, p_2, ..., p_n; \ p_i \geq 0, \ i = 1, 2, ..., n; \ \sum_{i=1}^{n} p_i = 1.$$

Sometimes, it is necessary to change these values $x_1, x_2, ..., x_n$
into a new form which is acceptable to the channel which we

want to use for transmission purposes. This task is accomplished by the process of coding.

Let us suppose that the code alphabet consists of a finite set $\mathscr{A} = \{a_1, a_2, ..., a_D\}$, $D \geq 2$. The elements of $\mathscr{A}$ are called *code characters*. Each symbol x_i is assigned a finite sequence of code characters called the *code word* assigned to x_i, $i = 1, 2, ..., n$. We assume that all the code words assigned to $x_1, x_2, ..., x_n$ are distinct. The collection of code words is called a *code* for X. The number of code characters in a code word is called the length of that code word.

Let $N_1, N_2, ..., N_n$ denote the lengths of code words assigned to $x_1, x_2, ..., x_n$ respectively. Then, the quantity [Shannon (1948)],

$$(1) \qquad L_1(<p_i>, <N_i>) = \sum_{i=1}^{n} p_i N_i$$

is called the *average code length of the code*. In general, one can construct more than one code for the given random variable X and then compute the average code length for each code. We assume that the channel through which the codes are being transmitted is *noiseless* so that the transmission is perfect. Usually, some cost is assigned with the transmission of a code character. If we assume that the cost of transmitting a code word is proportional to the length of the code word, then it is natural to select only that code word (for transmission purposes) which gives the least possible average code length.

This is the central problem in the theory of noiseless coding. To discuss this problem, in detail, we need some preliminary definitions.

Let us suppose that we have a random variable X which takes four distinct values x_1, x_2, x_3 and x_4 with probabilities

$$p_1, p_2, p_3 \text{ and } p_4; \ p_i \geq 0, \ i = 1, 2, 3, 4, \ \sum_{i=1}^{4} p_i = 1.$$

Consider the following code

x	Probabilities	Code
x_1	p_1	0
x_2	p_2	010
x_3	p_3	01
x_4	p_4	10

Then, it is easily seen that the binary sequence 010 could be decoded in three ways, namely; $x_2, x_3 x_1$ and $x_1 x_4$. This leads to an ambiguous situation which is not desirable. To overcome this sort of difficulty, we would like that a given string of code characters either cannot be decoded and if it can be decoded, then this can be decoded only in one way. If, such is the nature of the code for s, then we shall say that the code is **uniquely decipherable**. In other words, a code is *uniquely decipherable* if every sequence of code characters gives rise to at most one message. By a *message*, we shall mean a finite sequence consisting of values of X.

Let A_1 and A_2 be any two code words in a code for X. We say that A_1 is a *prefix* of A_2 if $A_2 = AC$ for some non—empty finite sequence C. Note that C need not be a code word. One way to be sure about a given code being uniquely decipherable is that no code word should be a prefix of another code word.

A code in which no code word is a prefix of another code word is said to be an irreducible or *instantaneous code*.

An instantaneous code is always uniquely decipherable. To prove it, let us consider a finite sequence of code characters and try to decode it by using the given instantaneous code. Begin from the left and continue till a code word W is obtained. If there is no such code word, then we say that the condition of unique decipherability is achieved vacuously. Since W cannot be the prefix of another code word, therefore, W corresponds to the first symbol of the message. Now continue towards the right until another code word is formed. Decode it. Continue this process till the whole sequence of code characters is exhausted.

The most commonly given example in this case is the following

X	Probabilities	Code
x_1	p_1	0
x_2	p_2	01

Clearly, this code is not instantaneous because the code word 0 is a prefix of the code word 01. However, if we are given any finite sequence of 0's and 1's, howsoever large it may be, it can always be decoded by noticing the positions of 1's in that. If we start from left and proceed to the right, then, we may have to wait for a long time before even we can form the first code word.

3.1.1 Coding Theorems for Shannon Entropy corresponding to Complete Random Variables

In this section, we shall confine ourselves only to uniquely decipherable codes. We prove the following theorem:

Theorem 1 *Let* X *be a random variable taking the values* $x_1, x_2, ..., x_n$ *with probabilities*

$$(1) \qquad p_1, p_2, ..., p_n; \ p_i \geq 0, \ i = 1, 2, ..., n; \ \sum_{i=1}^{n} p_i = 1.$$

Let $N_1, N_2, ..., N_n$ *denote the lengths of the code words assigned to* $x_1, x_2, ..., x_n$. *If the code is uniquely decipherable, then*

$$(2) \qquad \sum_{i=1}^{n} D^{-N_i} \leq 1,$$

$D \geq 2$ *denoting the number of code characters in the code alphabet.*

Proof. In the given uniquely decipherable code, let w_j denote the number of code words of length j and let r denote the maximum length. Then, it can be easily seen that

(3) $$\sum_{i=1}^{n} D^{-N_i} = \sum_{j=1}^{r} w_j D^{-j}$$

Let m be any positive integer chosen arbitrarily. Then,

(4) $$\left[\left[\sum_{j=1}^{r} w_j D^{-j} \right]^m \right.$$
$$\left. = \left[w_1 D^{-1} + w_2 D^{-2} + ... + w_r D^{-r} \right]^m \right.$$

Each term on the right hand side in (4) is of the form

$$\left[w_{i_1} D^{-i_1} \right] \left[w_{i_2} D^{-i_2} \right] ... \left[w_{i_m} D^{-i_m} \right]$$

where $1 \le i_1 \le r$, $1 \le i_2 \le r$,..., $1 \le i_m \le r$. Clearly, $m \le i_1 + i_2 + ... + i_m \le mr$. Hence (4) reduces to

$$\left[\sum_{j=1}^{r} w_j D^{-j} \right]^m = \sum_{j=m}^{mr} N(j) D^{-j}$$

where $N(j)$ is to be determined. Let us choose $i_1, i_2,...,i_m$ in this order. Then, we can start with any code word of length i_1, then follow it by any code word of length i_2, then follow it by any code word of length i_3 and so on... and end with any code word of length i_m. In this way, we get a sequence of code characters formed by juxtaposing the code words. Clearly, the number of sequence of length $i_1 + i_2 + ... + i_m = j$ is $w_{i_1} w_{i_2}...w_{i_m}$. Hence

$$N(j) = \sum_{i_1+i_2+..+i_m = j} w_{i_1} w_{i_2} ...w_{i_m}$$

where the sum is taken over all possible ways the integers $i_1,i_2,...,i_m$ can be written to form the total sum j. On the other, the total number of sequences of length j which can be formed by using the code characters of code alphabet having D distinct code characters is D^j. Hence

$$N(j) \leq D^j$$

so that

$$\left[\sum_{j=1}^{mr} w_j D^{-j}\right]^m = \sum_{j=m}^{mr} N(j)D^{-j} \leq \sum_{j=m}^{mr} 1$$

$$= mr - m + 1 \leq mr$$

Taking m^{th} root of both sides, we get $\sum_{j=1}^{r} w_j D^{-j} \leq m^{\frac{1}{m}} r^{\frac{1}{m}}$. Let $m \to \infty$ and using the fact that $m^{\frac{1}{m}} \to 1$ as $m \to \infty$, the conclusion follows.

The inequality (2) is due to Kraft (1949). Every uniquely

decipherable code satisfies it. Now we prove the following theorem.

Theorem 2   *Let $D \geq 2$ be a fixed positive integers and $N_1, N_2, ..., N_n$ be a set of positive integers satisfying the inequality (2). Then, there always exists a uniquely decipherable code with code words of lengths $N_1, N_2, ..., N_n$ for the random variable X.*

Proof   By a *tree* of *order* D and *size* k, we mean a system of points and lines such that each sequence s of length $\leq$ k, formed by using the elements of code alphabet A consisting of D distinct code characters, can be represented by a point V_s on it and if s^* is a sequence which can be obtained from s by adding a code character to it on the left or on the right and V_s^* is the point corresponding to s^* on the tree, then V_s and V_s^* can be joined to each other by a line.

Without any loss of generality, we may assume that $N_1 \leq N_2 ... \leq N_n-1 \leq N_n$. We are given that $\sum\limits_{i=1}^{n} D^{-N_i} \leq 1$. Then, we need the tree of order D and size N_n. Select a point on this tree corresponding to a sequence of length N_1. Discard all the $D^{N_n-N_1}$ terminal points which emanate from it. Since $\sum\limits_{i=1}^{n} D^{-N_i} \leq 1$, therefore, $\sum\limits_{i=1}^{n} D^{N_n-N_i} \leq D^{N_n}$. Thus, we have $D^{N_n-N_1} < D^{N_n}$. Hence at least one terminal point is left. Starting from this terminal point in the backward direction, we can choose a point on the tree corresponding to a sequence of length n_2 and then discard all the terminal points which emanate from it. Continue this process till we have chosen a point corresponding to a sequence of length N_n.

By the mode of our choice, it follows that the points chosen on the tree constitute an instantaneous code. Since every instantaneous code is uniquely decipherable, we have shown that we can find a uniquely decipherable code. This proves Theorem 2.

For a given random variable X, we can, in general, construct more than one uniquely decipherable code and then compute their average code lengths. From practical point of view, we would like to choose only that uniquely decipherable code for which the average code length is minimum. Up to what extent can we reduce the average code length? The answer to this question is given by the following theorem.

Theorem 3. *Let* X *be a random variable taking the values* $x_1, x_2, \ldots, x_n$ *with probabilities* $p_1, p_2, \ldots, p_n$; $p_n \geq 0$, $\sum_{i=1}^{n} p_i = 1$.

Let $\mathscr{A} = \{a_1, a_2, \ldots, a_D\}$, $D \geq 2$,

denote the code alphabet. Let N_i *denote the length of the code word assigned to the symbol* x_1, i = 1, 2, \ldots, n. *If the resulting code for* X *is uniquely decipherable, then*

$$(5) \qquad L_1(<p_i>, <N_i>) \geq \frac{H_n(p_1,p_2,\ldots,p_n)}{\log_2 D}$$

with equality in (5) *if and only if*

$$(6) \qquad p_i = D^{-N}, i = 1,2,\ldots,n.$$

Proof. Let $a_1,a_2,\ldots,a_n$ be positive numbers with

$$\sum_{i=1}^{n} a_i \leq 1.$$

Then by following the method used to prove 1.1.4 (9), it can be easily seen that

$$(7) \qquad -\sum_{i=1}^{n} p_i \log_2 p_i \leq -\sum_{i=1}^{n} p_i \log_2 a_i$$

with equality in (7) if and only if

$$(8) \qquad p_i = a_i, i = 1,2,\ldots,n.$$

Choose $a_i = D^{-N_i}$, $i = 1,2,\ldots,n$. Since the code under consideration is uniquely decipherable, therefore

$$\sum_{i=1}^{n} D^{-N_i} \leq 1.$$

Consequently, substituting $a_i = D^{-N_i}$ in (7) and carrying out the necessary calculations, we get

$$H_n(p_1,p_2,...,p_n) \leq L_1 (<p_i>, <N_i>) \log_2 D$$

from which (5) follows immediately. Since equality in (7) holds if and only if $p_k = a_k$, therefore, equality in (5) holds if and only if (6) holds. This completes the proof of Theorem 3.

The codes for which (6) holds are called absolutely optimal codes. In general, it is not necessary that all the probabilities $p_1,p_2,...,p_n$ are related to the corresponding code word lengths $N_1,N_2,...,N_n$. If there exists at least one value of i such that

$$p_i \neq D^{N_i},$$

then it is impossible to construct an absolutely optimal code for X because (6) is both necessary and sufficient condition in order that equality holds in (5). Under such circumstances, the only choice left with us is to construct a code which gives the minimum possible average code length. Such codes are called nearly optimal codes.

Theorem 3 tells us that it is impossible to construct a uniquely decipherable code for X for which the average code length is less than

$$\frac{H_n(p_1,p_2,..,p_n)}{\log_2 D}$$

It is desirable to devise uniquely decipherable codes for which the average length is close to the above. Thus we have

Theorem 4.

$$(9) \quad \begin{cases} \dfrac{H_n(p_1,p_2,\ldots,p_n)}{\log_2 D} \le L(<p_i>, <N_i>) \\[2ex] < \dfrac{H_n(p_1,p_2,\ldots,p_n)}{\log_2 D} + 1 \end{cases}$$

Proof Every uniquely decipherable code for X satisfies (5). If (6) holds, then (9) holds trivially. Also, in this case $N_i = \log_2 \frac{1}{p_i} / \log_2 D$ for each i and thus $\log_2 \frac{1}{p_i} / \log_2 D$ is a positive integer for each i. In any case, we can always find integers N_i such that

$$(10) \quad \frac{\log_2 \left(\frac{1}{p_i}\right)}{\log_2 D} \le N_i < \frac{\log_2 \left(\frac{1}{p_i}\right)}{\log_2 D} + 1, \ i = 1,2,\ldots,n.$$

Multiplying (10) by pi and summing with respect to i from 1 to n, we arrive at (9).

Theorem 4 tells us that the average code length can be brought within one digit of the lower bound set by Theorem 4. In fact, it is always possible to approach the lower bound as closely as desired. All that we have to do is to use block coding. In other words, construct suitably the code words for sequences of length s consisting of values of random variable X.

Let $L^{(s)}$ denote the average code length obtained when the sequences of length s are coded. Then, we can always construct a uniquely decipherable code such that

$$\frac{H_n{}_s(X^{(s)})}{\log_2 D} \leq L^{(s)} < \frac{H_n{}_s(X^{(s)})}{\log_2 D} + 1$$

where $X^{(s)} = (X_1, X_2, ..., X_s)$, $X_i = X$, $i = 1, 2, ..., s$, denotes s–dimensional random variable all of whose components are identically distributed. Since $X_1, X_2, ..., X_s$ are assumed independent, therefore $H_n{}_s(X^{(s)}) = s\, H_n(X^{(s)})$. Hence

$$\frac{H_n(X)}{\log_2 D} \leq \frac{L^{(s)}}{s} < \frac{H_n(X)}{\log_2 D} + 1$$

$$\lim_{s \to \infty} \frac{L^{(s)}}{s} = \frac{H_n(X)}{\log_2 D}$$

Thus, we have proved the following theorem.

Theorem 5. *Let X be a discrete random variable taking the values* $x_1, x_2, ..., x_n$ *with probabilities*

$$p_1, p_2, ..., p_n; \; p_i \geq 0, \; i = 1, 2, ..., n, \; \sum_{i=1}^{n} p_i = 1.$$

By suitably encoding, in a uniquely decipherable way, sufficiently long s–sequence consisting of values of X, it is always possible to make the $L^{(s)}/s$, the average code length per value of X, as close to $H_n(X)$ as desired. There does not exist any uniquely decipherable code whose average code length is less than $H_n(X)$ where $H_n(X)$ denotes the Shannon entropy with base 2, and D denotes the number of code characters in the code alphabet.

So far, we have made use of the Shannon entropy only. Since we have other entropies also, therefore, it is natural that we should try to establish similar coding theorems for other entropies.

3.1.2. Coding Theorems for Shannon Entropy corresponding to Incomplete Random Variables

In the previous section, we have restricted ourselves only to complete random variables. Now we shall discuss some coding theorems concerning incomplete random variables.

In probabilistic coding theory, this is a new area of research and, as far as the author knows, the first attempt in this direction has been made by Nath (1976).

Rényi (1960) introduced the concepts of incomplete and generalized random variables. He put forward the idea that if some of the events are not observable, then the resulting random variable, if finite and discrete, will be incomplete in the sense that it will take a number of values smaller than the actual number of values it would have taken theoretically and, thus, the sum of the associated probabilities will be strictly less than one. A random variable which is either complete or incomplete is said to be a generalized random variable.

Let X be a generalized random variable taking values with probabilities

$$p_1, p_2, \ldots, p_n; \ p_i \geq 0, \ 0 < \sum_{i=1}^{n} p_i \leq 1.$$

Let A denote the code alphabet with $D \geq 2$ distinct code characters and let N_i denote the length of the code word assigned to the value x_i, $i = 1, 2, \ldots, n$. In case $0 < \sum_{i=i}^{n} p_i < 1$, then it is clear that at least one value of X is observable and the values $x_1, x_2, \ldots, x_n$ are then the observable values and the only alternative left is to devise code words only for those values of X which are observable. As an obvious generalization of 3.1(1), it is natural to define the average code length as

(1) $$\hat{L}_1(<p_i>, <N_i>) = \sum_{i=1}^{n} p_i N_i \ / \ \sum_{i=1}^{n} p_i$$

If $\sum_{k=1}^{n} p_k = 1$, then (1) reduces to 3.1 (1). The definition (1) is quite a natural one in the sense that we are looking upon $\hat{L}_1(<p_i>, <N_i>)$ as the ordinary weighted average of the lengths $N_1, N_2, \ldots, N_n$, the weights being the probabilities $p_1, p_2, \ldots, p_n$. If $N_1 = N_2$, then $\hat{L}(<p_i>, <N_i>) = N$. We prove the following theorem, due to Nath (1976):

Theorem 1 *Let there be a generalized random variable* X *taking the values* $x_1, x_2, ..., x_n$ *with probabilities*

$$p_1, p_2, ..., p_n; \; p_i \geq 0, \; 0 < \sum_{i=1}^{n} p_i \leq 1.$$

Suppose these values are assigned code words by using symbols from a code alphabet $\mathscr{A}$ *having* $D \geq 2$ *distinct code characters and* N_i *denotes the length of the code word assigned to the symbol* x_i, $i = 1, 2, ..., n$. *If the code for* X *is uniquely decipherable, then*

$$(2) \qquad \begin{aligned} & \hat{L}_1(<p_i>, <N_i>) \\ \\ & \geq -\frac{\sum\limits_{i=1}^{n} p_i \log_2 p_k}{\sum\limits_{i=1}^{n} p_i} + \log_2\left[\sum\limits_{i=1}^{n} p_i\right] \end{aligned}$$

with equality in (2) *if and only if*

$$(3) \qquad p_i = D^{-N_i}\left[\sum_{j=1}^{n} p_j\right], \; i = 1, 2, ..., n$$

Proof Let us choose

$$q_1, q_2, ..., q_n; \; q_i \geq 0, \; i = 1, 2, ..., n; \; 0 < \sum_{i=1}^{n} q_i \leq 1.$$

Then, by 3.1.1 (7), we have

(4)
$$-\sum_{i=1}^{n}\left(\frac{p_i}{\sum_{j=1}^{n}p_j}\right)\log_2\left(\frac{p_i}{\sum_{j=1}^{n}p_j}\right)$$

$$\leq\sum_{i=1}^{n}\left(\frac{p_i}{\sum_{j=1}^{n}p_j}\right)\log_2\left(\frac{q_i}{\sum_{j=1}^{n}q_j}\right)$$

which, on simplification, gives

(5)
$$-\sum_{i=1}^{n}p_i\log_2 p_i\left/\sum_{i=1}^{n}p_i\right.$$

$$\leq-\left[\sum_{i=1}^{n}p_i\log_2 q_i\left/\sum_{i=1}^{n}p_i\right.\right]+\log_2\left[\sum_{i=1}^{n}q_i\left/\sum_{i=1}^{n}p_i\right.\right]$$

Choosing $q_i = D^{-N_i}$, $i = 1,2,...,n$, and proceeding exactly as in Theorem 1 of 3.1.1, Theorem 1 now follows immediately.

Rényi (1960) defined that

(6)
$$H_n(p_1,p_2,...,p_n) = -\left[\sum_{i=1}^{n}p_k\ \log_2\ p_i\left/\sum_{i=1}^{n}\ p_i\right.\right],$$

$$(p_1,p_2,...,p_n)\in\Delta_n$$

which is a generalization of the Shannon entropy. Hence, (2) may be written in the form

$$(7) \qquad \hat{L}_1(<p_i>, <N_i>) = \frac{H_1(p_1,\ldots,p_n)}{\log_2 D} + \log_2\left[\sum_{i=1}^{n} p_i\right]$$

The presence of the term $\log_2\left[\sum_{i=1}^{n} p_i\right]$ in(2) and (7) takes a little bit away from the original version of Theorem 3 of 3.1.1 for complete random variable. P. Nath proposed that this awkward situation can be overcome by introducing the new concept of strongly decipherable codes.

Definition 1 *Let X be a generalized random variable taking the values $x_1, x_2, \ldots, x_n$ with probabilities $p_1, p_2, \ldots, p_n$, $p_i \geq 0$, $0 < \sum_{i=1}^{n} p_i \leq 1$. Suppose we assign code words to these values of X by using code characters from a code alphabet $\mathscr{A}$ consisting of $D \geq 2$ distinct code characters. Let N_i denote the length of the code word assigned to the value x_i, $i = 1, 2, \ldots, N$. Then the resulting code for X will be said to be strongly decipherable if it satisfies the inequality*

$$(8) \qquad \sum_{i=1}^{n} G^{-N_i} \leq \sum_{i=1}^{n} p_i.$$

The inequality (8) is weaker than 3.1.1 (2) and we know that every uniquely decipherable code satisfies 3.1.1 (2). However, this does not mean that every strongly decipherable code is also a uniquely decipherable code. But every strongly decipherable can be made a strongly decipherable code.

A major difference between 3.1.1 (2) and (8) is that whereas the former is purely combinatoric and does not involve the probabilities, the latter one is both combinatoric and probabilistic as both the probabilities and the code words lengths appear in it.

In probabilistic coding theory, in order to minimize the cost of transmission, it is customary to assign shorter code words to messages (or symbols) which occur with larger probabilities. Now, the following theorem can be proved easily by making use of (5).

Theorem 2 *Let* X *be a generalized random variable taking the values* $x_1, x_2, ..., x_n$ *with probabilities*

$$p_1, p_2, .. p_n; p_i \geq 0; \; 0 < \sum_{i=1}^{n} p_i \leq 1.$$

Suppose the values of X *are assigned code words by using symbols from a code alphabet* $\mathscr{A}$ *consisting of* $D \geq 2$ *distinct code characters and* N_i *is the length of the code word assigned to the symbol* x_i, $i = 1, 2, ..., n$. *If the resulting code for* X *is strongly decipherable in the sense that it satisfies* (8), *then*

$$(9) \qquad \begin{cases} \hat{L}_1(<p_i>, <N_i>) \geq \dfrac{H_n(p_1, p_2, ..., p_n)}{\log_2 D}, \\[2mm] (p_1, p_2, ..., p_n) \in \Delta_n \end{cases}$$

with equality if and only if 3.1.1(6) *is satisfied.*

Following the arguments needed to prove Theorem 3 in 3.1.1, it can be easily seen that the average code word lengths N_i can always be constrained by the inequalities 3.1.1 (10) and then, it can be concluded that there always exists a *strongly decipherable code* satisfying the inequality

$$(10) \qquad \begin{cases} \dfrac{H_n(p_1,p_2,...,p_n)}{\log_2 D} \le \hat{L}_1(<p_i>, <N_i>) \\ < \dfrac{H_n(p_1,p_2,...,p_n)}{\log_2 D} + 1. \end{cases}$$

Finally, the following theorem can be proved exactly in the same way as we have proved Theorem 5 in 3.1.1.

Theorem 3 *Let there be a random variable* X *taking the values* $x_1, x_2, ..., x_n$ *with probabilities*

$$p_1, p_2, ..., p_n; \; p_i \ge 0, \; 0 < \sum_{i=1}^{n} p_i \le 1.$$

Let $\mathscr{A}$ *denote the code alphabet having* $D \ge 2$ *distinct code characters. By encoding in a strongly decipherable way, sufficiently long sequences consisting of values of* X, *it is possible to make the average code length per value of* X *as close to* $H_n(p_1, p_2, ..., p_n)$, $(p_1, p_2, ..., p_n) \in \Delta'_n$, *as desired. It is not possible to find a strongly decipherable code whose average code length is less than* $H_n(p_1, p_2, ..., p_n)$.

It may be noted that, in Theorem 3, it is not possible to replace the condition of strong decipherability, but unique decipherability. For example, let us consider the case $D = 2$. Consider the following example:

X	Probability	Code words	Lengths
x_1	0.50	1	1
x_2	0.20	01	2

Then $p_1 + p_2 = 0.70$. $\sum_{i=1}^{2} 2^{-N_i} = 2^{-1} + 2^{-2} = 0.50 + 0.25$ $= 0.75$.

Thus the code is uniquely decipherable but not strongly decipherable. Also

$$H_2(p_1, p_2) = \frac{0.96}{0.75} \text{ and } L_1(<p_i>, <N_i>) = \frac{0.90}{0.70}$$

so that

$$H_2(p_1, p_2) > L_1(<p_i>, <N_i>).$$

This is, indeed, an interesting situation for incomplete probability distribution. From these observations, it is obvious that if we want to develop probabilistic coding theory for generalized random variables, then the coding must be done in a strongly decipherable way rather than uniquely decipherable way.

3.1.3 Shannon—Wolfowitz Coding Theorem

Wolfowitz's strong converse of Shannon's coding theorem is indispensable in information theory since an information transmitting channel does not have a capacity when corresponding entropy function admits a wide domain. The construction of such a domain is given in this section following Behara (1973).

Let us consider an information channel with code alphabet

$$\mathscr{A} = \{a_1, a_2, ..., a_l\}$$

and output code alphabet

$$\mathscr{B} = \{b_1, b_2, ..., b_m\}$$

A finite sequence of code letters is called a code word. Let X and Y denote input and output random variables respectively and their joint probability distribution is given by

$$P\{X=a_i, Y=b_j\} = p(a_i, b_j) = p_{ij}, \forall i, \forall j.$$

The joint entropy is given by

$$H(X, Y) = -\sum_i \sum_j p_{ij} \log p_{ij}.$$

The marginal and conditional entropies denoted by $H(X)$, $H(Y)$ and $H(X/Y)$, $H(Y/X)$ may be readily given. A channel is described as a system for sending codes and the channel probability is given by

$$p(b_i/a_j), i = 1,2,...,l, j = 1,2,....m.$$

The information processed by it is given by

$$I(X/Y) = H(X) - H(X/Y),$$

whereas its capacity is defined as

$$C = \max I(X/Y),$$

the maximum being taken over the input probabilities.

Now let $\mathfrak{B}$ denote the N–partition of the set of output words such that, in the absence of an error probability, the ith input word should belong to the ith partition almost surely. A code (N,n,λ) is defined as a set of N input words, each of length n, such that its maximum error probability is at most equal to λ. N is called the length of the code. A permissible transmission rate R (≥ 0) for the channel is defined if $\exists$ (N,n,λ_n) where $N = [2^{nR}]$ such that

$$\lim_{n \to \infty} \lambda_n \to 0.$$

The capacity C for the channel is given by sup R. Thus, for any $\epsilon > 0$, if $R = C - \epsilon$, it would be possible to maintain the transmission rate with small λ, whereas, if $R = C + \epsilon$, it would not be possible to maintain the transmission rate with small λ. In fact, in the latter case,

$$\lim_{n \to \infty} \lambda_n = 1.$$

In order to define the capacity of a channel we need the coding theorem and its strong converse due to Shannon and Wolfowitz respectively. As Wolfowitz (1964) states it, a number C which enters into the lower and the upper bounds on the lengths of possible codes (N,n,λ), $0 < \lambda < 1$ for any channel is called the capacity of the channel. Shannon's theorem states that for any $\epsilon > 0$, there exists a code $(2^{n(C-\epsilon)}, n, \lambda_n)$ such that

$$\lim_{n \to \infty} \lambda_n = 0.$$

Wolfowitz's theorem states that for any $\epsilon > 0$ there does not exist a code $(2^{n(C+\epsilon)}, n, \lambda_n)$ with arbitrarily small λ_n, as $n \to \infty$. In order to demonstrate that Wolfowitz's theorem must hold for a channel to have capacity, we now describe the concept of λ–capacity due to Wolfowitz.

Let $N(n,\lambda)$ be the longest code length for a discrete channel. The λ—capacity of a channel is then defined by

$$C(\lambda) = \lim_{n \to \infty} \sup \frac{1}{n} \log N(n,\lambda), \; 0 < \lambda < 1.$$

Wolfowitz (1963) states that $C(\lambda) = C$, a constant for all $\lambda \in (0,1)$ where C is called the capacity of the channel. Violation of this statement would then establish the channel to be without a capacity.

The channel probability for a channel, due to Ash (1965), is given by

$$[(n+1) \binom{n}{i}]^{-1}, \; (i = 0,...,n).$$

Our theorems, given below without proofs, shows that the channels of the above type are without capacity as they violate Wolfowitz's above statement. Ash's theorem [Ash (1965)] is a special case of ours.

Consider a unit square bounded by the lines $\lambda = 0$, $Y = 0$, $\lambda = 1$, $Y = 1$. Let Γ be a ray of lines radiating downward from (1,1) bounded by $2Y - \lambda - 1 = 0$ and $\epsilon Y - \lambda + 1 = 0$ for arbitrarily small $\epsilon > 0$. Let Δ be a ray of lines radiating upward from (1,0) bounded by $2Y + \lambda - 1 = 0$ for arbitrarily small $\epsilon > 0$.

THEOREM 1. *For a given $\gamma_0 \in \Gamma$, $\exists$ a $\lambda_0 = \lambda_0(\gamma_0)$ such* that

$$\lim_{\lambda_0 < \lambda \uparrow 1} C_{\gamma_0}(\lambda) = 1, \; \gamma_0 \in \Gamma,$$

where $\quad C_{\gamma_0}(\lambda) \geq 1 - H(\gamma_0).$

THEOREM 2. *For a given $\delta_0 \in \Delta$, $\exists$ a $\lambda_0 = \lambda_0(\delta_0)$ such* that

$$\lim_{\lambda \downarrow \lambda_0} C_{\delta_0}(\lambda) = 0, \; \delta_0 \in \Delta,$$

where $\quad C_{\delta_0}(\lambda) \leq 1 - H(\delta_0).$

Finally, it can be proved that the Wolfowitz theorem holds for this channel iff $C(\lambda) = C$ for all $\lambda \in (0,1)$. Thus, the Wolfowitz theorem becomes as fundamental as the Shannon theorem in information theory since the channel is shown to be without a capacity, when the Wolfowitz theorem fails to hold.

For an application of the Shannon–Wolfowitz theorem on the expected value of the distortion and the upper bound of the code length in terms of rate distortion measure for indecomposable channels [Behara (1966)], we proceed as follows:

If any product of i, i = 1,2,..., a, stochastic matrices is indecomposable, the underlying channel is said to be indecomposable. Thus any n–sequence, which is the same as an above product , is stochastic indecomposable aperiodic. Here an attempt has been made to define a measure of distortion between the transmitted and received n–sequences appropriate to indecomposable channels. Then the Shannon–Wolfowitz Theorem on the expected value of the distortion and the upper bound of the code length in terms of rate distortion measure (which is monotonically decreasing function of distortion measure) is shown to apply for indecomposable channels.

3.2 CODING THEOREY FOR RENYI ENTROPY

In this section, we shall discuss some coding theorems concerning the Rényi entropy. The first attempt in this direction was made by Campbell (1965).

Campbell (1965) pointed out that it is good to use 3.1 (1) as a measure of average code length when the cost of using a code word of length N_i is directly proportional to N_i. If the cost of encoding and decoding equipment were also an important factor, then the possibility is not ruled out that the cost may turn out to be more nearly an exponential function. Hence, in some cases, it might be more appropriate to choose a code which minimizes the quantity $\sum_{i=1}^{n} p_i D^{t^N i}$, D denoting the size of the code alphabet. Here the average code length is of order t as given below:

$$(1) \qquad \begin{cases} L_t(<p_i>, <N_i>) = t^{-1} \log_D \left[\sum_{i=1}^{n} p_i D^{t^N i} \right], \\ 0 < t < \infty \end{cases}$$

and then try to minimize it rather than $\sum_{i=1}^{n} p_i D^{t^N i}$ It can be easily seen that

$$\lim_{t \to 0} L_t(<p_i>, <N_i>) = \sum_{i=1}^{n} p_i N_i$$

so that the average length 3.1 (1) may be regarded as average code length of order zero. If $N_i = N$ for all $i = 1,2,...,n$, then $L_t(<p_i>, <N_i>) = N$ which is intuitively expected too. It is for this reason that it is better to minimize the right hand side of (1) rather than $\sum_{i=1}^{n} p_i D^{t^N i}$. Now we prove the following theorem:

Theorem 1 *Let X be a random variable taking the values* $x_1, x_2, ..., x_n$ *with probabilities*

$$p_1, p_2, ..., p_n; \ p_i \geq 0, \ \sum_{i=1}^{n} p_i = 1.$$

Suppose the values of X are encoded by using the letters of a code alphabet having $D \geq 2$ *distinct letters. Let* N_i *denote the length of the code word assigned to* x_i, $i = 1,2,...,n$. *If the code for X is uniquely decipherable, then*

(2) $\qquad L_t(<p_i>, <N_i>) \geq {}^{\alpha}H_n(p_1,p_2,...,p_n), \ \alpha > 0.$

where

(3) $\qquad \alpha = \dfrac{1}{1 + t}, \ 0 < t < \infty.$

    Proof For $t = 0$ and $\alpha = 1$, we have 3.1.1 (5). Let $0 < t < \infty$. We need Holder's inequality

(4) $\qquad \displaystyle\sum_{i=1}^{n} x_i y_i \geq \left[\sum_{i=1}^{n} x_i^{p} \right]^{1/p} \left[\sum_{i=1}^{n} y_i^{q} \right]^{1/q}$

where $1/p + 1/q = 1$, $p < 1$, the equality in (4) holding if and only if

(5) $\qquad \begin{cases} \dfrac{x_1^{p}}{y_1^{q}} = \dfrac{x_2^{p}}{y_2^{q}} = ... = \dfrac{x_n^{p}}{y_n^{q}}, \\[2mm] x_i > 0, \ y_i > 0; \ i = 1,2,...,n. \end{cases}$

    Since zero probabilities do not change the LHS and RHS of (2), it is enough to assume that all $p_i > 0$, $i = 1,2,...,n$. Choose

$\qquad \begin{cases} x_i = (p_i)^{\frac{1}{t}} D^{-N_i}, \ y_i = (p_i)^{\frac{1}{t}}, \\[2mm] i = 1,2,...,n; \ p = -t, \ q = 1-\alpha \end{cases}$

Since $\frac{1}{p} + \frac{1}{q} = 1$, therefore, we must have $-\frac{1}{t} + \frac{1}{1-\alpha} = 1$ which gives $\alpha = \frac{1}{t+1}$. Substitution in (4) gives

$$(6) \qquad \left[\sum_{i=1}^{n} p_i D^{t^{N_i}}\right]^{-\frac{1}{t}} \left[\sum_{i=1}^{n} p_i^{\alpha}\right]^{\frac{1}{1-\alpha}} \leq \sum_{i=1}^{n} D^{-N_i}$$

with equality if and only if

$$(7) \qquad \left\{ \begin{array}{l} \dfrac{p_1 D^{t^{N_1}}}{p_1^{\alpha}} = \dfrac{p_2 D^{t^{N_2}}}{p_2^{\alpha}} = \cdots = \dfrac{p_n D^{t^{N_n}}}{p_n^{\alpha}} \\[4mm] = \dfrac{\sum\limits_{i=1}^{n} p_i D^{N_i}}{\sum\limits_{i=1}^{n} p_i^{\alpha}} \end{array} \right.$$

The inequality (6) may be written in the form

$$(8) \qquad \left[\sum_{i=1}^{n} p_i D^{t^{N_i}}\right]^{\frac{1}{t}} \geq \frac{\left[\sum\limits_{i=1}^{n} p_i^{\alpha}\right]^{\frac{1}{1-\alpha}}}{\sum\limits_{i=1}^{n} D^{-N_i}}$$

Since the code is uniquely decipherable, therefore,

$$\sum_{i=1}^{n} D^{-N_i} \leq 1 \Rightarrow \frac{1}{\sum\limits_{i=1}^{n} D^{-N_i}} \geq 1 \,.$$

Hence (8) yields

$$(9) \qquad \left[\sum_{i=1}^{n} p_i \, D^{tN_i} \right]^{\frac{1}{t}} \geq \left[\sum_{i=1}^{n} p_i{}^{\alpha} \right]^{\frac{1}{1-\alpha}}$$

from which (2) follows immediately. This proves our theorem.

Now let us examine as to when equality in (2) holds. We claim that equality in (2) holds if and only if

$$(10) \qquad D^{-N_i} = \frac{p_i{}^{\alpha}}{\displaystyle\sum_{j=1}^{n} p_j{}^{\alpha}} , \; i = 1,2,\ldots,n.$$

Let us suppose that (10) holds. Then

$$
\begin{aligned}
L_t(<p_i>, <N_i>) \;\; &= \frac{1}{t} \log \left[\sum_{i=1}^{n} p_i \, D^{tN_i} \right] , \; 0 < t < \infty \\[2mm]
&= \frac{\alpha}{1-\alpha} \log \sum_{i=1}^{n} p_i \left(\frac{p_i{}^{\alpha}}{\displaystyle\sum_{j=1}^{n} p_j{}^{\alpha}} \right)^{\frac{\alpha-1}{\alpha}} \\[2mm]
&= \frac{\alpha}{1-\alpha} \log \left\{ \sum_{i=1}^{n} p_i{}^{\alpha} \Big/ \left[\sum_{j=1}^{n} p_j{}^{\alpha} \right]^{\frac{\alpha-1}{\alpha}} \right\} \\[2mm]
&= \frac{\alpha}{1-\alpha} \log \left[\sum_{j=1}^{n} p_i{}^{\alpha} \right]^{\frac{1}{\alpha}} \\[2mm]
&= \frac{1}{1-\alpha} \log \left[\sum_{i=1}^{n} p_i{}^{\alpha} \right]
\end{aligned}
$$

Now suppose equality holds in (2). Then

$$(11) \qquad \left[\sum_{i=1}^{n} p_i D^{t N_i} \right]^{\frac{1}{t}} = \left[\sum_{i=1}^{n} p_i^{\alpha} \right]^{\frac{1}{1-\alpha}}$$

Then (8) givers $\sum_{i=1}^{n} D^{-N_i} \geq 1$. But, by unique decipherability $\sum_{i=1}^{n} D^{-N_i} \leq 1$. Hence $\sum_{i=1}^{n} D^{-N_i} = 1$. Now (11) gives

$$\begin{aligned} \frac{\sum_{i=1}^{n} p_i D^{t N_i}}{\sum_{i=1}^{n} p_i^{\alpha}} &= \frac{\left[\sum_{i=1}^{n} p_i^{\alpha} \right]^{\frac{t}{1-\alpha}}}{\sum_{i=1}^{n} p_i^{\alpha}} = \frac{\left[\sum_{i=1}^{n} p_i^{\alpha} \right]^{\frac{1}{\alpha}}}{\sum_{i=1}^{n} p_i^{\alpha}} \\ &= \left[\sum_{i=1}^{n} p_i^{\alpha} \right]^{\frac{1}{\alpha} - 1} = \left[\sum_{i=1}^{n} p_i^{\alpha} \right]^{t} \end{aligned}$$

Then, substitution in (7) yields (10).

From (10), it follows that

$$(12) \qquad \begin{cases} N_i = - \alpha \log_D p_i + \log_D \left[\sum_{j=1}^{n} p_j^{\alpha} \right], \\ \alpha > 0, \quad \alpha \neq 1 \end{cases}$$

Now we can prove the following theorem.

Theorem 2 *Let* $\alpha = \dfrac{1}{1+t}$ *,* $0 < t < \infty$*. By encoding sufficiently long sequences consisting of values of* X*, in a* *uniquely decipherable way, it is possible to make the average code length of order t per value of X as closely to* $^{\alpha}H_n(p_1,p_2,..,p_n)$ *as we desire. It is not possible to find a uniquely decipherable code whose average code length of order t is less than* $^{\alpha}H_n(p_1,p_2,...,p_n)$.

Proof Let N_s denote the length of the code word assigned to a sequence of length s. Choose N_s such that

$$\left[\begin{array}{l} -\alpha \log P(s) + \log \left[\sum_{i=1}^{n} p_i{}^{\alpha}\right]^s \leq N_s \\ < 1-\alpha \log P(s) + \log \left[\sum_{i=1}^{n} p_i{}^{\alpha}\right]^s \end{array}\right.$$

where $P(s)$ denote the probability of the sequence of length s. Then, it can be easily seen that $\sum_{s} D^{-N_s} \leq 1$ so that unique decipherability is guaranteed. Then, it follows that

$$[P(s)]^{-\alpha t} \left[\sum p_i{}^{\alpha}\right]^{st} \leq D^{tN_s} < D^t [P(s)]^{-\alpha t} \left[\sum p_i{}^{\alpha}\right]^{st}$$

from which it follows that

$$\left[\sum p_i{}^{\alpha}\right]^{(1+t)s} \leq \sum_{s} P(s) D^{tN_s} < D^t \left[\sum p_i{}^{\alpha}\right]^{1+t}$$

which gives

$$^{\alpha}H_n{}^s (X^{(s)}) \leq L_t{}^{(s)} < {}^{\alpha}H_n{}^s (X^{(s)}) + 1$$

where $L_t^{(s)}$ denotes the average code length of order t per s—sequence of values of X. Since Rényi entropy is additive, we have ${}^{\alpha}H_n^s(X) = s\,{}^{\alpha}H_n(X)$. Hence

$$ {}^{\alpha}H_n \leq \frac{L_t^{(s)}}{s} < \frac{{}^{\alpha}H_n}{s} + \frac{1}{s} $$

Making $s \to \infty$, we arrive at the conclusion.

A code for which equality holds in 3.1.1 (5) is called an absolutely optimal code. Obviously 3.1.1 (6) is the necessary and sufficient condition for a code to be optimal. As it is obvious, 3.1.1 (6) is a relationship between p_i's and N_i's and, as such, it does not depend upon the Shannon entropy $H_1(p_1, p_2, ..., p_n)$.

A careful examination of (2) shows that the orders of the average code length and the Rényi entropy are not the same. In fact, they are connected by (3). One way of making the order of average code length and that of Rényi entropy is to define

(13) $\qquad \ell_{\alpha} = L_t.$

Then (2) reduces to

$$ \ell_{\alpha} \geq {}^{\alpha}H_n(p_1, p_2, ..., p_n), \ \alpha > 0 $$

but, even then, we are not able to conclude that equality (13) holds if and only if 3.1.1 (6) holds. Hence the question arises. How should we define average code length $L_{\alpha}^{*}(<x_i>, <N_i>)$ such that

(14) $$L_{\alpha}^{*}(<p_i>, <N_i>) \geq {}^{\alpha}H_n(p_1, p_2, ..., p_n)$$

with equality in (14) if and only if 3.1.1 (6) holds? This question was raised and answered by Nath (1975). He defined the average code length as

(15) $$\mathscr{L}(<p_i>, <N_i>, f, \phi) = \phi^{-1}\left(\frac{\sum_{i=1}^{n} f(p_i)\phi(N_i)}{\sum_{i=1}^{n} f(P_i)}\right)$$

where f is a non—constant positive—valued continuous function defined on (0,1), ϕ is a strictly monotonically increasing and continuous real—valued function defined on $[1,\infty)$, and ϕ^{-1} denotes the inverse function of ϕ. From (15), it is evident that in fact we are defining the average code length as the most general quasi linear mean—value rather than an ordinary weighted average.

In order to determine exactly the forms of (15), one needs to make some more natural assumptions based on intuition. One of the intuitive requirements which any measure of average code length should satisfy is that it should be translative for all positive integers, This simply means that if we increase the length of each code word by a positive integer m by attaching to the right of each code word finite sequences of length m constructed by using the code characters, then, the average code length must increase by m. Thus, we get the functional equation.

$$(16) \quad \left[\phi^{-1} \left(\frac{\sum\limits_{i=1}^{n} f(p_i)\phi(N_i+m)}{\sum\limits_{i=1}^{m} f(P_i)} \right) = \phi^{-1} \left(\frac{\sum\limits_{i=1}^{n} f(pi)\phi(N_i)}{\sum\limits_{i=1}^{n} f(p_i)} \right) + m, \right.$$
$$m = 1, 2, 3, \ldots$$

The functional equation (16) is known as translativity equation. Aczel (1974) showed that the only forms of ϕ admissible in (16) can be $\phi = \phi_1$ and $\phi = \phi_\alpha$, $\alpha > 0$, $\alpha \neq 1$, where

$$(17) \qquad \phi_1(x) = bx + a, b > 0$$

$$(18) \qquad \phi_\alpha(x) = bD^{(\alpha-1)x} + a, D \geq 2, (\alpha-1)b > 0.$$

In the first case, we get

$$\mathscr{L}(<p_i>, <N_i>, f, \phi) = \mathscr{L}(<p_i>, <N_i>, f, \phi_1)$$

where

$$(19) \qquad \mathscr{L}(<p_i>, <N_i>, f, \phi_1) = \sum_{i=1}^{n} f(p_i)N_i \Big/ \sum_{i=1}^{n} f(p_i).$$

In the latter case,

$$\mathscr{L}(<p_i>, <N_i>, f, \phi) = \mathscr{L}(<p_i>, <N_i>, f, \phi_\alpha)$$

where

(20)

$$
\begin{cases}
\mathscr{L}(<p_i>, <N_i>, f, \phi_\alpha) \\[2mm]
= (\alpha-1)^{-1} \log \left(\dfrac{\sum\limits_{i=1}^{n} f(p_i)\, D^{(\alpha-1)N_i}}{\sum\limits_{i=1}^{n} f(p_i)} \right), \; \alpha \neq 1. \\[4mm]
= (\alpha-1)^{-1} \log \left(\sum\limits_{i=1}^{n} f(p_i) D^{(\alpha-1)N_i} \right) \\[4mm]
+ (1-\alpha)^{-1} \log \sum\limits_{i=1}^{n} f(p_i), \; \alpha \neq 1.
\end{cases}
$$

We now restrict to $\alpha > 0$, $\alpha \neq 1$, and then choose f such that

(21) $$\sum_{i=1}^{n} f(p_i) = \sum_{i=1}^{n} p_i^{\alpha}, \; \alpha > 0, \; \alpha \neq 1.$$

It can be easily proved that all the continuous solutions of

(21), for all positive integers n, are only of the form $f(p) = p^{\alpha}$, $p \in [0,1]$, $\alpha > 0$, $\alpha \neq 1$ so that $\mathscr{L}(<p_i>, <N_i>, f, \phi_\alpha)$ reduces to $\mathscr{L}(\alpha)$ where

(22)

$$
\begin{cases}
\mathscr{L}(\alpha) = (\alpha-1)^{-1} \log_D \left[\sum\limits_{i=1}^{n} p_i\, D^{(\alpha-1)N_i} \Big/ \sum\limits_{i=1}^{n} p_i^{\alpha} \right], \\[4mm]
\alpha > 0, \; \alpha \neq 1
\end{cases}
$$

The measure of average code length $\mathscr{L}(\alpha)$ is due to Nath (1975). It is not a straight forward generalization of

$L_t(<p_i>,<N_i>)$. If we put $t = \alpha-1$, then $L_t(<p_i>,<N_i>)$ does not reduce to $\mathscr{L}(\alpha)$. On the other hand,

$$\lim_{\alpha \to 1} \mathscr{L}(\alpha) = L_1(<p_i>,<N_i>).$$

Now we are able to prove the following theorem due to Nath (1975).

Theorem 3 *Let* X *be a random variable taking the values* $x_1, x_2, ..., x_n$ *with probabilities*

$$p_1, p_2, ..., p_n; \; p_i \geq 0, i = 1, 2, ..., n; \; \sum_{i=1}^{n} p_i = 1.$$

Let $\mathscr{A}$ *denote the code alphabet having* $D \geq 2$ *distinct code characters. Let us encode the values of* X *by using code characters from* $\mathscr{A}$. *If the code is uniquely decipherable and* N_i *denotes the length of the code word assigned to* x_i, $i = 1, 2, ..., n$; *and further the average code length* $\mathscr{L}(\alpha)$ *of order* $\alpha > 0$, $\alpha \neq 1$, *is defined by* (22), *then*

(23) $$\mathscr{L}(\alpha) \geq \frac{{}^{\alpha}H_n(p_1, p_2, ..., p_n)}{\log_2 D}, \; \alpha > 0, \; \alpha \neq 1$$

with equality in (23) if and only if 3.1.1 (6) holds. The Rényi entropy in (23) is calculated with base 2.

Before we prove the above theorem, we would like to mention that if $\alpha \to 1$, then (23) reduces to 3.1.1 (5) with equality if and only if 3.1.1 (6) holds. By making use of

Holder's inequality, it can be easily seen that for $\alpha > 1$

$$(24) \qquad \sum_{i=1}^{n} p_i{}^{\alpha} q_i{}^{1-\alpha} \leq 1,$$

with equality if and only if $p_i = q_i$ for all $i = 1,2,...,n$. The inequality in (24) is reversed for $0 < \alpha < 1$. Let us choose

$$(25) \qquad q_i = \frac{D^{-Ni}}{\sum\limits_{j=1}^{n} D^{-Nj}} , \, i = 1,2,...,n.$$

Then, from (24) and (25), we obtain

$$(26) \qquad \frac{\sum\limits_{i=1}^{n} p_i{}^{\alpha} D^{(\alpha-1)Ni}}{\left[\sum\limits_{j=1}^{n} D^{-Nj} \right]^{1-\alpha}} \geq 1, \, \alpha > 1$$

with equality if and only if

$$(27) \qquad p_i = \frac{D^{-Ni}}{\sum\limits_{j=1}^{n} D^{-Nj}}, \, i = 1,2,...,n.$$

From (26), we get

$$\frac{\sum\limits_{i=1}^{n} p_i{}^{\alpha} D^{(\alpha-1)Ni}}{\sum\limits_{i=1}^{n} p_i{}^{\alpha}} \geq \frac{\left[\sum\limits_{i=1}^{n} D^{-Nj} \right]^{1-\alpha}}{\sum\limits_{i=1}^{n} p_i{}^{\alpha}}$$

from which it follows that

$$\left[(\alpha-1) \ \log_D \ \left[\sum_{i=1}^{n} \ p_i^{\alpha} \ D^{(\alpha-1)N_i} \middle/ \ \sum_{i=1}^{n} \ p_i^{\alpha}\right]\right.$$
$$\left.\geq \frac{^{\alpha}H_n(p_1,p_2,\ldots,p_n)}{\log_2 D} - \log_D \sum_{j=1}^{n} D^{-N_j}\right]$$

which may be written in the form

$$(28) \qquad \frac{^{\alpha}H_n(p_1,p_2,\ldots,p_n)}{\log_2 D} \leq \mathscr{L}(\alpha) + \log_D \left[\sum_{j=1}^{n} D^{-N_j}\right], \ \alpha > 1.$$

Similarly, for $0 < \alpha < 1$, it can be proven that

$$(29) \qquad \left[\frac{^{\alpha}H_n(p_1,p_2,\ldots p_n)}{\log_2 D} \leq \mathscr{L}(\alpha) + \log_D \left[\sum_{j=1}^{n} D^{-N_j}\right],\right.$$
$$\left.0 < \alpha < 1\right.$$

Combining (28) and (29), we conclude that

$$(30) \qquad \left[\frac{^{\alpha}H_n(p_1,p_2,\ldots,p_n)}{\log_2 D} \leq \mathscr{L}(\alpha) + \log_D \left[\sum_{j=1}^{n} D^{-N_j}\right],\right.$$
$$\left.\alpha > 0, \ \alpha \neq 1.\right.$$

Since the code under consideration is uniquely decipherable, therefore, $\sum_{j=1}^{n} D^{-N_j} \leq 1$ and hence $\log_D \left[\sum_{j=1}^{n} D^{-N_j}\right] \leq 0$. Consequently, from (30), the inequality (23) follows immediately.

Now we show that equality in (23) holds if and only if (6) of 3.1.1 holds. If the latter holds, then it is easy to see that $\mathscr{L}(\alpha)$ reduces to $\dfrac{^{\alpha}H_n(p_1, p_2, ..., p_n)}{\log_2 D}$. Now, suppose that equality holds in (23). Then, we get

$$\log \sum_{j=1}^{n} D^{-N_j} \geq 0 \Rightarrow \sum_{j=1}^{n} D^{-N_j} \leq 1.$$

But, using decipherability, $\sum_{j=1}^{n} D^{-N_j} \leq 1$. Hence, we have $\sum_{j=1}^{n} D^{-N_j} \leq 1$ and then (27) reduces to (6) of 3.1.1. This cmpletes the proof of Theorem 3.

By following the arguments given after Theorem 3, in 3.1.1 it follows now that we can constrain the lengths N_j, i=1,2,...,n, by the inequalities 3.1.1 (9). If $\alpha > 1$, then 3.1.1 (9) yields

$$1 \leq p_i{}^{\alpha-1} D^{(\alpha-1)N_i} < D^{\alpha-1}$$

from which it follows that

$$\left[\begin{aligned} &\frac{^{\alpha}H_n(p_1, p_2, .., p_n)}{\log_2 D} \leq \mathscr{L}(\alpha) < \frac{^{\alpha}H_n(p_1, p_2, .., p_n)}{\log_2 D} + 1, \\ &\alpha > 1. \end{aligned} \right.$$

On the similar lines, it can be established that

$$
\left[
\begin{array}{l}
\dfrac{{}^{\alpha}H_n(p_1,p_2,..,p_n)}{\log_2 D} \leq \mathscr{L}(\alpha) \leq \dfrac{{}^{\alpha}H_n(p_1,p_2,..,p_n)}{\log_2 D} + 1, \\[2mm]
0 < \alpha < 1.
\end{array}
\right.
$$

Thus, we have the following theorem due to Nath (1975):

Theorem 4 *Let* X *be a random variable taking the values* $x_1,x_2,...,x_n$ *with probabilities*

$$
p_1,p_2,...,p_n; \; p_i \geq 0, \; \sum_{i=1}^{n} p_i = 1.
$$

Let $\mathscr{A}$ *denote the code alphabet having* $D \geq 2$ *distinct characters. Then, there always exists a uniquely decipherable code satisfying the inequality*

$$
(31) \qquad \dfrac{{}^{\alpha}H_n(p_1,p_2,..,p_n)}{\log_2 D} \leq \mathscr{L}(\alpha) < \dfrac{{}^{\alpha}H_n(p_1,p_2,..,p_n)}{\log_2 D} + 1.
$$

The inequality (31) tells us that it is always possible to bring the average code length $\mathscr{L}(\alpha)$ of order $\alpha > 0$, $\alpha \neq 1$, within one digit of the greatest lower bound set by Theorem 3. This advantage is not possessed by $L_t(<p_i>, <N_i>)$. By following the arguments needed to prove Theorem 3, in 3.1.1 the following theorem due to Nath (1975) can now be proved easily:

Theorem 5 *Let* X *be a random variable taking the values* $x_1, x_2, \ldots, x_n$ *with probabilities*

$$p_1, p_2, \ldots, p_n; \; p_i \geq 0, \sum_{i=1}^{n} p_i = 1,$$

and let $\mathscr{A}$ denote the code alphabet consisting of D $\geq$ 2 *distinct code characters. By suitably encoding in a uniquely decipherable way sufficiently long sequences consisting of values of* X, *it is possible to make the average code length of order* α *as close to* $^{\alpha}H_n(X)$ *as desired. It is not possible to devise a uniquely decipherable code for which the average code length of order* α *is less than* $^{\alpha}H_n(X)$.

3.3 CODING THEORY FOR POLYNOMIAL ENTROPY

It seems that the first attempt to discuss coding theorem using the polynomial entropy $^\beta h_n$ was made by Nath and Mittal (1973).

Let us consider the mappings $^\alpha \Psi_D : \mathbb{R} \to \mathbb{R}$ defined as

$$(1a) \qquad ^\alpha \Psi_D(x) = \frac{1 - D^{(1-\alpha)x}}{1 - D^{1-\alpha}}, \; \alpha \neq 1;$$

(1b) $\qquad ^{\alpha}\Psi_D(x) = x, \alpha = 1.$

Then, it can be easily seen that

(2) $\qquad ^{\alpha}\Psi_D(\Re(\Delta_n)) = \mathfrak{B}(\Delta_n) \equiv {}^{\beta}h_n,$

where $\Re(\Delta_n) \equiv {}^{\alpha}H_n$ and $\mathfrak{B}(\Delta_n) \equiv {}^{\beta}h_n$ denote n—dimensional Rényi and polynomial entropies respectively. Also,

(3) $\qquad ^{1}\Psi_D(H_n(p_1,p_2,...,p_n)) = H_n(p_1,p_2,...,p_n).$

Equation (2) shows the connection between the Rényi entropy and polynomial entropy ${}^{\beta}h_n$.

To discuss the coding theorems concerning polynomial entropy ${}^{\beta}h_n$ one has to define suitably a measure or the measures of average code length so that the desired theorems hold. One such measure of average code length

(4) $\qquad \begin{cases} \ell_{\beta}(<p_i>,<N_i>) = 1 - \dfrac{\left[\sum\limits_{i=1}^{n} p_i^{\beta} \Big/ \sum\limits_{i=1}^{n} p_i^{\beta} \, D^{(\alpha-1)N_k}\right]}{1 - 2^{(1-\beta)}}, \\ \beta \neq 1, \beta > 0. \end{cases}$

was proposed by Nath and Mittal (1973). It seems that they did not characterize it by using any intuitive ideas. However, it has been pointed out to me by P. Nath that, for D = 2,3,...

(5) $\qquad {}^{\beta}\Psi_D(\mathscr{L}(\beta)) = \ell_{\beta}, \ \beta > 0, \ \beta \neq 1.$

In other words, the relationship between $\mathscr{L}(\alpha)$ and $\ell(\alpha)$ is of the same form as that between ${}^{\alpha}H_n(p_1,p_2,...,p_n)$ and ${}^{\beta}h_n(p_1,p_2,...,p_n)$. Now we prove the following theorem [Nath and Mittal (1973)]:

Theorem 1 *Let X be a random variable taking the values* $x_1,x_2,...,x_n$ *with probabilities*

$$p_1,p_2,...,p_n; \ p_i \geq 0, \sum_{i=1}^{n} p_i = 1.$$

Let $\mathscr{A}$ be a code alphabet having $D \geq 2$ distinct code characters. Let N_i denote the length of the code word assigned to x_i, $i = 1,2,...,n$. If the code is uniquely decipherable, then

(6) $\qquad \ell(\beta) \geq {}^{\beta}h_n(p_1,p_2,...,p_n), \ \beta > 0, \ \beta \neq 1.$

where

(7) $\qquad {}^{\beta}h_n(p_1,p_2,...,p_n) = \dfrac{\sum\limits_{i=1}^{n} p_i^{\beta} - 1}{D^{1-\beta} - 1}, \ \beta > 0, \ \beta \neq 1.$

Proof We give the proof only for $\beta > 1$. The proof for the case $0 < \beta < 1$ follows on similar lines. By (26) of 3.2 we get, for $\beta > 1$,

$$(8) \quad \frac{1 - \sum\limits_{i=1}^{n} p_i^{\beta}}{1 - D^{1-\beta}} \leq \frac{1 - \left[\sum\limits_{i=1}^{n} p_i^{\beta}\left[\sum\limits_{i=1}^{n} D^{-N_i}\right]^{1-\beta} \sum\limits_{i=1}^{n} p_i^{\beta} D^{(\beta-1)N_k}\right]}{1 - D^{1-\beta}}$$

and it can be easily seen that (8), indeed, also holds for all $0 < \beta < 1$. Using the fact that since the code is uniquely decipherable, therefore, $\sum\limits_{i=1}^{n} D^{-N_i} \leq 1$, and we get, from (8), the inequality (6).

It can be easily seen that if $p_i = D^{-N_i}$, $i = 1,2,...,n$; then $\ell(\beta)$ reduces to (7). On the other hand, if equality holds in (6), then (8) gives $\sum\limits_{i=1}^{n} D^{-N_i} \geq 1$. But, because of unique decipherability, $\sum\limits_{i=1}^{n} D^{-N_i} \leq 1$. Hence, $\sum\limits_{i=1}^{n} D^{-N_i} = 1$ and consequently (27) of 3.2 gives $p_i = D^{-N_i}$, $i = 1,2,...,n$. Thus, we conclude that equality in (6) holds if and only if (6) of 3.1.1 holds.

It may be noted that we are trying to retain (6) of 3.1.1 which is, in fact, a condition for the absolute optimality of the code. Once, this is done, it is possible to constrain the lengths N_i, $i = 1,2,...,n$; by the inequalities (10) of 3.1.1 irrespective of the fact as to whether the entropy under consideration is additive or nonadditive. Campbell (1965) did not retain (6). Instead, he gave (12) of 3.2 which contains the parameter α.

Not much is known in connection with the coding theorems concerning polynomial entropy $\beta h_n(p_1, p_2, \ldots, p_n)$.

It is our intention to formulate coding theorems for all measures of entropy derived geometrically or algebraically in a general setting and study their effects on the construction of error—correcting codes.

REFERENCES

Aczel, J. (1964). Ein Eindeutigkeitssatz in der Theorie der Funktionalgleichungen und einige ihrer Anwendungen. *Acta Math. Acad. Sci. Hungar.*, *15*, 355–362.

Aczel, J. (1966). *Lectures on Functional Equations and Their Applications*. Academic Press, New York.

Aczel, J. and Daroczy, Z. (1963). Charakterisierung der Entropien positiver Ordnung und der Schannonschen Entropie. *Acta Math. Acad. Sci. Hungar.*, *14*, 95–121.

Aczel, J. and Daroczy, Z. (1975). *On Measures of Information and Their Characterization.* Academic Press, New York.

Arimoto, S. (1971). Information–theoretical Considerations on Estimation Problems. *Information and Control, 19,* 181–194.

Ash, R. (1965). A Simple Example of a Channel for which the Strong Converse Fails. *IEEE Trans. Inform. Theory, IT–11,* 456–457.

Behara, M. (1966). Approximating Theorem for Indecomposable Channels. *International Congress of Mathematicians (Moscow), Information Bulletin, 10,* 4.

Behara, M. (1968). Entropy as a Measure of Utility in Decision Theory. *Invited Paper presented at the Math. Forschungsinstitut, Oberwolfach.*

Behara, M. (1973). Shannon–Wolfowitz Coding Theorem of Information Theory. *Selecta Statistica Canadiana, 1,* 79–82.

Behara, M. (1974). Entropy and Utility. *Information, Inference and Decision,* (ed. G. Menges). *Theory and Decision Library, 1,* 145–154. [D. Reidel, Dordrecht].

Behara, M. (1985). Polynomial Entropy. *Contributions to Econometrics and Statistics Today,* (ed. H. Schneeweiss and H. Strecker), 46–51. [Springer–Verlag, Berlin].

Behara, M. and Chawla, J.M.S. (1975). Generalized Gamma–Entropy. *Selecta Statistica Canadiana, 2,* 15–38.

Behara, M. and Chawla, J.M.S. (1979). Shannon and Polynomial Entropies as Semivaluations on Lattices. *Statistische Hefte*, *20*, 197–203.

Behara, M. and Chorneyko, I.Z. (accepted). On Some Trigonometric Entropies. Journal of the Orissa Mathematical Society.

Behara, M. and Kofler, E. (1982). Forecasting under Linear Partial Information. *Time Series Methods in Hydrosciences, Developments in Waterscience*, *17*, 608–614. [Elsevier, Amsterdam].

Behara, M., Kofler, E. and Menges, G. (1978). Entropy and Informativity in Decision Situations under Partial Information. *Statistische Hefte*, *19*, 124–130.

Behara, M. and Nath, P. (1970). *Additive and Non–Additive Entropies of Finite Measurable Partitions*. McMaster Mathematical Report, *31*. [Mathematical Reviews, *42*: 4322].

Behara, M. and Nath, P. (1973). Additive and Non–Additive Entropies of Finite Measurable Partitions. *Lecture Notes in Mathematics*, *296*, 102–138. [Springer–Verlag, Berlin].

Behara, M. and Nath, P. (1974). Information and Entropy of Countable Measurable Partitions – I. *Kybernetika*, *10*, 491–503.

Behara, M. and Nath, P. (1980). On Additive and Non–Additive Measure of Directed Divergence. *Kybernetika*, *16*, 1–12.

Behara, M. and Nath, P. (submitted). On Classification of Entropies: Subadditivity and Pseudo–Subadditivity.

Boltzmann, L. (1896). *Vorlesungen ueber Gastheorie.* J.A. Barth, Leipzig.

Bose, R.C. (1939). On the Construction of Balanced Incomplete Block Designs. *Ann. Eugenics, 9,* 353–399.

Campbell, L.L. (1965). A Coding Theorem and Rényi's Entropy. *Information and Control, 8,* 423–429.

Chawla, J.M.S. (1974). *Entropies and the Isomorphism Problem for Bernoulli Shifts.* Ph.D. Thesis, Math. Dept., McMaster University, Canada.

Fadeev, D.K. (1956). On the Concept of Entropy of a Finite Probabilistic Scheme (Russian). *Uspehi Mat. Nauk* (N.S.), *11,* No.1 (67), 227–231.

Golay, M.J.E. (1949). Notes on Digital Coding. *Proc. IRE, 37,* 657.

Guiasu, S. (1977). *Information Theory with Applications.* McGraw–Hill, New York.

Hamming, R.W. (1950). Error Detecting and Error Correcting Codes. *Bell System Tech. J., 29,* 147–160.

Hardy, G.H., Littlewood, J.E. and Polya, G. (1952). *Inequalities,* 2nd edition. Cambridge University Press, London.

Hartley, R.V. (1928). Transmission of Information. *Bell System Tech. J., 7,* 535–563.

Havrda, J. and Charvat, F. (1967). Quantification Method of Classification Processes. Concept of Structural α–Entropy. *Kybernetika, 3,* 30–35.

Kannappan, Pl. (1974). On a Functional Equation Connected with Generalized Directed–Divergence. *Aequationes Math.*, *11*, 51–56.

Khinchin, A.I. (1953). The Concept of Entropy in the Theory of Probability (Russian). *Uspehi Mat. Nauk*, *8*, No. 3 (55), 3–20.

Kraft, L.G. (1949). *A Device for Quantizing, Grouping and Coding Amplitude Modulated Pulses.* M.S. Thesis, Electrical Eng. Dept., MIT, U.S.A.

Lee, P.M. (1964). On the Axioms of Information Theory. *Ann. Math. Stat.*, *35*, 415–418..

Nath, P. (1975). On a Coding Theorem Connected with Rényi's Entropy. *Information and Control*, *29*, 234–242.

Nath, P. (1976). Some Theorems on Noiseless Coding. *Information and Control*, *32*, 355–367.

Nath, P. and Mittal, D.P. (1973). A Generalization of Shannon's Inequality and its Application in Coding Theory. *Information and Control*, *23*, 439–445.

Rényi, A. (1960). On Measures of Entropy and Information. *Proc. 4th Berkeley Symp. Math. Stat. Probability, 1960, 1*, 547–561.

Shannon, C.E. (1948). A Mathematical Theory of Communication. *Bell System Tech. J.*, *27*, 379–423; 623–656.

Tverberg, H. (1958). A New Derivation of the Information Function. *Math. Scand.*, *6*, 297–298.

Wiener, N. (1948). *Cybernetics, or Control and Communication in the Animal and the Machine.* Herman, Paris; Technology Press MIT, Cambridge, Mass.; Wiley, New York.

Wolfowitz, J. (1957). The Coding of Messages Subject to Chance Errors. *Illinois J. Math.*, *1*, 591–606.

Wolfowitz, J. (1963). On Channels Without Capacity. *Information and Control*, *6*, 49–54.

Wolfowitz, J. (1964). *Coding Theorems of Information Theory*, 2nd edition. Springer–Verlag, Berlin.

Zaanen, A.C. (1958). *An Introduction to the Theory of Integration.* North–Holland, Amsterdam.